One Left

One Left

A NOVEL

Kim Soom

Translated by Bruce and Ju-Chan Fulton

Foreword by Bonnie Oh

UNIVERSITY OF WASHINGTON PRESS

Seattle

One Left is published with the support of the Literature Translation Institute of Korea (LTI Korea).

한명 (One left)
by Kim Soom
First published in 2016 by Hyundae Munhak Co., Ltd., Korea
© Kim Soom
All rights reserved
English-language edition © 2020 by the University of Washington Press
Translation © 2020 by Bruce and Ju-Chan Fulton

This English-language edition was published by arrangement with the University of Washington Press through HAN Agency Co., Korea.

Design by Katrina Noble
Composed in Arno Pro, typeface designed by Robert Slimbach

24 23 22 21   5 4 3 2

Printed and bound in the United States of America

UNIVERSITY OF WASHINGTON PRESS
uwapress.uw.edu

LIBRARY OF CONGRESS CATALOGING-IN-PUBLICATION DATA
LC record available at https://lccn.loc.gov/2020006819
LC ebook record available at https://lccn.loc.gov/2020006820

ISBN 978-0-295-74765-1 (hardcover), ISBN 978-0-295-74766-8 (paperback),
ISBN 978-0-295-74767-5 (ebook)

Cover illustration: *Copsychus saularis*, Plate 27, Oriental magpie-robin, watercolor by Margaret Bushby Lascelles Cockburn from her *Neilgherry Birds and Miscellaneous* (1858). Natural History Museum, London, UK. Bridgeman Images.

Frontispiece: *Sonyŏ sang* (Statue of a girl), created by Kim Seo-kyung and Kim Eun-sung. Photo courtesy of Choi Ho Shik.

The paper used in this publication is acid free and meets the minimum requirements of American National Standard for Information Sciences—Permanence of Paper for Printed Library Materials, ANSI Z39.48–1984.∞

FOREWORD

Bonnie Oh

The story, *One Left*, takes place in some future time when there are no known surviving comfort women except for a *hidden* one. Hence the title of the novel, *One Left*. The one left is referred to only as "she."

She is 93 years old and lives alone with a cat, named Nabi (butterfly), in a dilapidated house on a nearly abandoned narrow street, 15-*bŏnji* (15th Street). The alley has neither trees nor potted plants, only empty houses, ready to be torn down for redevelopment. One morning she turns on her TV as she starts her morning chores, folding the faded blanket and wiping the warped floors, and she hears that the last of the surviving comfort women is about to die. She mutters, "And then there's me!" She is about to step down into the yard when she sees a dead magpie next to her shoes, almost hidden, obviously Nabi's offering to her to please her. She doesn't like Nabi doing that and cringes. The lifeless bird transports her to her childhood home. Her ears are ringing with her mom's voice, crying and pleading with her younger siblings to go find their oldest sister because the magpie is howling and her firstborn has not returned from the river.

She was 13 and was gathering marsh snails on the riverbank. She was grabbed by men, thrown into a truck that sped away and then stopped at Taegu to load more girls, and was put on a train that raced in what appeared to be a northerly direction—seemingly indefinitely. After several days, disheveled and dirty, the girls boarded an open-back truck and were delivered to a building encircled by barbed-wire fence. It was May but felt like winter. It was Manchuria, which was a Japanese puppet state, little different from a colony. When she fell to the ground, six marsh snails were still squirming in her hand. That was more than seventy years ago, but she still feels the snails tickling her palm. On the train, she met other girls of similar age. All thought, claimed, or imagined they were headed for some place nice, where they could earn money to send home: Kunja going to a thread factory; Hanok, a couple of years older, to a needle factory; Aesun to someplace wonderful . . .

❋

Nabi's yowling brings her back to reality. But everything she sees or touches reminds her of the incidents and friends at the comfort station. She remembers the Japanese officer who struck a match to Haegŭm's pubic hair, the soldier who stabbed Kisuk in the thigh, the screams and pleas of girls begging for their lives. To her, the past and present are merged, with the past being more vivid. She murmurs and repeats, in order not to forget, their names as they come to mind: Kisuk ŏnni,[1] Hanok ŏnni, Hunam ŏnni, Haegŭm . . . Kŭmbok ŏnni, Suok ŏnni, Punsŏn . . . Aesun, Tongsuk ŏnni, Yŏnsun, Pongae, Sŏksun ŏnni. . . . The girl sitting next to her on the train was Kisuk ŏnni. Sundŏk, Hyangsuk, Myŏngsuk ŏnni, Kunja, Pokcha ŏnni, T'anshil, Changshil ŏnni, Yŏngsun, Miok ŏnni. . . . And then there were Japanese names: Umeko, Kiyoko, Fumiko, Eiko, Kinoe, Asako . . . , randomly given by the station manager and by soldiers after they were finished with business. She herself had a dozen Japanese names and more than one Korean name. But her real name? She hasn't heard it in a long, long time.

᠅

One Left is the first Korean novel devoted exclusively to the subject of the comfort women. As the number of surviving victims dwindled, Kim Soom became concerned that the true details and extent of their horrific experiences would be lost—once all of them died. By the time the novel was published in 2016, a quarter century had elapsed since Kim Haksun had shocked the world by disclosing that she had been a comfort woman. Although the comfort women issue had immediately become an energetic national movement, the Korean public became weary of it due to the prolonged, unsuccessful effort of demanding that Japan take responsibility. The author felt urgently that the comfort women's *real, excruciatingly painful* experiences might be forgotten unless depicted in a personal narrative.

Kim Soom's novel rebuts denials of the validity of the comfort women's claims by synthesizing an intense personal story with painstaking historical research. For the author, a novel became a fitting form to describe the true nature and scope of the cruelties these victims endured. Their accounts were often dismissed as inconceivable and too brutal to be real. In fact, a basis of Japanese denial is that "Japanese people could not possibly have done it." It was not enough to describe in plain text that these young women were raped thirty to forty times a day. Kim Soom needed to graphically illustrate what happened to the young women's private parts after being raped so many times and what happened to the young women when they could not satisfy the soldiers' relentless demands: their swollen vaginas were slid open with swords, were pierced with nails or with heated metal rods.

One Left is not born purely of the author's creative imagination but is based on her exhaustive research and careful reading of the comfort women's testimonies. To render credibility, Kim Soom appends hundreds of endnotes, commenting on virtually every episode and name in a book of just 268 pages in the Korean-language version. By exposing what happened to these women in extreme detail, Kim transcends testimonies and historical records to capture the gut-wrenching suffering of the victims.

※

The term *comfort women* is a euphemism for *sex slaves* of the Imperial Japanese military during World War II, or the Pacific War, in Asia from 1931 to 1945. An estimated two hundred thousand[2] young women and girls were "recruited" in a variety of ways—deception, coercion, and abduction—and confined in "comfort stations" in China, Manchuria, and other Pacific-region countries, including Australia. The ages of the kidnapped girls ranged from as young as 11 to 25 or older. Of those, 80 percent were Koreans, because Korea—the entire peninsula—was then Japan's colony, and Japanese men supposedly preferred Korean women to those of other nationalities. Most were from destitute rural areas, especially from Kyŏngsang Province. Poverty was endemic in colonial Korea, contrary to recent Japanese claims that Japan had developed the Korean economy and later laid the foundation for the South Korean economic "miracle on the Han."

These young women and girls were raped by tens of Japanese soldiers a day. Soldiers in the afternoons and the officers in the evenings lined up in queues outside the girls' stalls, which were divided by fabric or plywood panels. The slightest insubordination resulted in severe punishments, beatings, deprivation of food and medicines, isolation. When they became pregnant, their babies were taken and their uteruses taken out altogether. Women who could not be cured of gonorrhea or syphilis were removed from the site and never seen again.

At the war's end many were slaughtered on site or thrown from aboard ships on return trips to their home countries[3]—to eradicate the evidence. Only twenty thousand survived. Some returned to their native lands; others remained where they were, hiding, not knowing for years that Japan had been defeated. Many who reached their home countries led hidden lives, eking out a living working various service jobs. Few married and fewer could bear children. The few who did saw their children suffer serious health problems, from brain diseases, to muscular problems, to early death due to the mothers' previous venereal disease infections.

For decades these women remained silent as the world swept history under the rug. The Japanese government concealed it to the best of its ability. In the Cold War era, Japan was geographically and ideologically on the front line of the anti-Communist struggle, and the United States coddled its former enemy for fear of offending it. The US even preserved Japan's Imperial system despite the fact that Emperor Hirohito had been directly involved in all military activities, including establishment of the comfort women system. Gen. Douglas MacArthur reneged on his own early judgment and released war criminals, including Kishi Nobusuke, the maternal grandfather of the current right-wing Japanese prime minister, Shinzo Abe.

In 1987 the decades-long military dictatorship in Korea came to an end, ushering in the *minjung*, or "popular democracy." Two scholars, Yoon Chung-ok of Korea and Yoshimi Yoshiaki of Japan,[4] unearthed materials on comfort women and published their work. Finally, the decades-old Cold War and the Soviet Union ended within the span of two years, 1989–91. These events converged to create an atmosphere favorable for supporters of comfort women to persuade Kim Haksun to break the silence on August 14, 1991. She opened the floodgates, sending a tidal wave across the globe. One former comfort woman after another appeared, and a total of 238 registered with the South Korean government. Later in the fall, the Korean Council for Justice and Remembrance for the Issues of Military Sexual Slavery by Japan (formerly, the Korean Council for the Women Drafted for Military Sexual Slavery by Japan) was established. In the following year, Dongwoo Lee Hahm, then a World Bank employee, founded the Washington Coalition for Comfort Women Issues (WCCW) in the United States.

Since 1992, the comfort women movement has mounted efforts to build a support system for the victims, establishing places of residence and providing government stipends. Activists have also brought suits against Japan (all of them lost) and have presented demands to the Japanese government: to acknowledge the existence of and official involvement in the system and to offer an *official* apology and compensation. Other related activities have emerged: weekly noontime demonstrations (held on Wednesdays), running for nearly three decades, in front of the Japanese embassy in Seoul; academic conferences and symposiums across the United States and abroad; and statues and memorials erected to honor the comfort women. There are more than ten in the United States and several others across the globe, including in Germany, Australia, China, the Philippines, and South Korea. The United Nations has declared that crimes against comfort women are crimes against humanity and a violation of human rights, and it has passed resolutions calling for Japan to meet the victims' demands.

Also impressive is the growth and expansion of interest in the subject in academia. After the first academic conference in 1996 at Georgetown University,[5] countless such gatherings have been held all over the world. A significant number of young scholars are pursuing graduate studies on the subject.[6]

After half-hearted cooperation and a few personal apologies from *individual* prime ministers in the early 1990s, Japan is now denying nearly all aspects of the issue and calling comfort women professional prostitutes. The Japanese government has spent more than half a billion dollars to incentivize its overseas residents and diplomats to engage in obstructionist activities.

In December 2015 the South Korean government reached an oral, irreversible agreement with the Japanese government. The victims, supporters, and a majority of the Korean public condemned the accord and refused to recognize it. The relationship between Korea and Japan is at its worst in years, with no prospect for an easy or quick resolution.

※

She, the last one, is back at the house, which is closer to demolition. Nearly half of the empty houses on 15-*bŏnji* have been razed. After a fitful night of sleep, she turns on the TV. She hears that the last of the 238 registered has not yet died but is barely hanging on, hooked up to a respirator and trying to speak, "I'm Yun Kŭmshil." Haltingly and out of breath, the dying woman continues, "I can't allow myself to die—not with no one after me to speak . . ."

Wiping tears that have welled up, she, the silent and hidden one, makes a decision. She is going to see the *last one*—to assure herself that she's still here and that she'll tell it all.

As she boards the minibus dressed in her best pink cardigan, a name flutters onto her tongue: P'unggil. It is her name—her real name that she had forgotten.

She is P'unggil, 13 years old, and she is the one left.

BONNIE OH was born and raised in South Korea. She is emerita distinguished professor of Korean studies at Georgetown University, where she served as director of the women's studies program. She has published extensively on comfort women during World War II, the American military government in Korea, as well as on nationalism and feminism in Korea.

NOTES

1   *Ŏnni* means "older sister" in an honorable way, not necessarily meaning related.
2   After publication of *Chinese Comfort Women* by Peipei Qiu of Vassar (Oxford, UK: Oxford University Press, 2014), the estimate doubled to four hundred thousand because the previously closed and vast country of China was opened to research.
3   Tomiyama Taeko, "At the Bottom of the Pacific," in *Silenced by History* (Tokyo: Gendai Kikaushitsu, 1995), 44.
4   Yoshimi Yoshiaki is a professor of Japanese modern history at Chuo University in Tokyo. He is a founding member of the Center for Research and Documentation on Japan's War Responsibility and author of *Sexual Slavery in the Japanese Military during World War II* (New York: Columbia University Press, 2000).
5   Margaret Stetz and I were co-conveners. The proceedings from this conference and additional material were edited and published five years after the meeting as *Legacies of Comfort Women of World War II* (Armonk, NY: M. E. Sharpe, 2001). It turned out to be the first academic book on comfort women.
6   Between 1995 and 2005, forty-six PhD dissertations were written on the topic. See Frank Joseph Shulman, chapter 8 in *Comfort Women: A Movement for Justice and Women's Rights in the United States* (forthcoming).

One Left

PROLOGUE

S HE PICKS UP a seed and eyes it intently until she can almost see the tiny thing sucking her up. Once inside the pore-sized seed, she will never be found.

But maybe the gods too would consider me dirty?

She wonders what expression God would wear if He were to look down on her just then. *Would He frown? Glower? Shrug? Would He look on me with pity? Does God have a face anyway? And does it get old like ours?* [1]

Before she turned 14, her life was over, she had no future.

She's seized by a sudden urge to disgorge all.
I want to tell it, then die. [2]

1

Now there's only one left. Yesterday there were two, but one of them passed away overnight.

She hears this from the television as she's folding her blanket, and her fingers go numb. *Wasn't it just a month ago that one of the last three passed?* The synthetic blanket used to be the color of a tangerine, but now it's faded to apricot.

Setting the folded blanket aside, she wipes the floor with her hand and gathers the dust and the bits of thread and flakes of skin and strands of gray hair into a tiny ball.

"And then there's me!" she mutters.

⁂

Leaving the television on, she goes out to the veranda. As she's about to step down to the yard, she flinches. A dead magpie, beak tucked beneath a wing, lies next to her copper-colored shoes.

Nabi, her cat. Four days ago it brought her a baby sparrow, tiny and feeble as a newborn's untouched hand. Yes, the birdie she saw practicing aerial maneuvers in the alley. Over and over it soared and plunged down the obscure, sunless alley devoid of trees and plants. When she ventured near, the mother sparrow shrilled an emergency alert from her lookout somewhere aloft. The startled birdie was gone in a flash, as if sucked into a rain gutter. All she wanted was to enjoy its amazing tricks, but no, she realized forlornly, to the sparrows she was a terrible presence.

She sits huddled at the edge of the veranda, legs draped over the edge, looking back and forth at the dead magpie and her shoes. It's odd how the more she looks the harder it is to tell them apart.

Nabi is nowhere to be seen. Sometimes the cat announces its presence with plaintive yowling, otherwise it makes its prowl unheard and unseen. There's only the dwindling supply of food and water in the plastic bowls she sets out that tells her it's visited. It's a stray she found lingering by the faucet. She fed the emaciated creature some anchovies left over from broth and that's how they connected.

Are alley cats the only creatures that offer their prey to their master rather than consuming it themselves? They're like war trophies, the mice and birds Nabi leaves on display next to her shoes. Like today's offering, the first such gift was also a dead magpie. *Take it back!* Unfazed by the tongue-lashing, the cat sprawled out instead on the cement surface of the yard and the following day deposited another gift next to her shoes. This time a mouse.

It knows I get the jitters seeing the results of its hard work! She cringes at the thought of the cat offering its kill just to please her.

Today's prey is more frightening and ominous—because she's just heard that another one has passed?

The ash-gray beak of the magpie is open the width of a small grape, revealing the crimson inside. As if someone spit a drop of blood there.

She wonders if Nabi caught it in the first light of dawn.

❊

She extends her right foot toward the shoe at the base of the veranda, only to jerk it back, realizing her foot was targeting the magpie instead. As she approaches the faucet her head perks up—in the alley a magpie is calling. She imagines the cawing issuing not from its vocal cords but from the tip of the beak that's been pecking at earthworms and digging into mouse guts.

Her younger sisters were summoned by their mother every time they heard a magpie. One day she, the oldest girl, left to gather marsh snails and never came back. When after a year she was still missing, Mother began calling to the younger girls, "Go see where that magpie is!"

"But why, Mother?" the girls would ask.

"Maybe that's where your big sister's body is."

At the call of a magpie Mother would stop what she was doing, whether stoking the firebox or dipping soy sauce from the crock pot in the yard, and tell the girls to go find it.

The girls shrank like violets and dared not approach the magpie. But Mother would insist, and then Number Two would put on her act, going instead to the sweet potato patch and returning to report that Ŏnni wasn't there.

If her mother were still alive she'd want to ask, *For goodness' sake, why didn't you go look yourself instead of sending my poor little sisters?*[1]

When five years had passed and her oldest girl hadn't returned, Mother picked half a dozen ears of corn from their kitchen garden and went to see the fortune teller who lived out behind the tobacco patch. "She crossed the sea and she's dead and gone."[2] Hearing this, Mother adopted a nightly ritual of setting out three bowls of water—one on the soy sauce crock, one on the crock of fermented soybean paste, and one on the crock of hot pepper paste—and bowing to each.[3] No matter that the soybean paste crock was empty, the soybean mash that would have filled it having been nibbled up already by the hungry girls.[4]

Father was a day laborer whose earnings couldn't keep the family fed day in and day out. Mother for her part was never able to memorize the Oath of Imperial Subjects—a necessary condition for obtaining food rations from the colonial administration. So she scrounged the dregs left when others crushed their soybeans for oil and fed them to the children. And when she put in a day at the local treadmill, she gathered the chaff, added radish greens to it, and made porridge.

The insistent cries of the magpie remind her of her mother saying, "Go see where that magpie is." But if she were to go to where the magpie is calling now, surely what she would find is she herself—a girl without a stitch of clothing on her bony body, her ankles lashed together by a soldier's belt.

The soldier's eyes were the color of pus. When she tried to escape his clutches, he undid his belt and the next she knew, he'd tied her ankles together.[5] And when she closed her eyes in resignation, he assumed she was dozing off and slapped her back and forth. Eyes snapping open, she looked daggers at the man's red-hot, contorted face; it had turned so strange and scary.

The soldiers who visited her body, each and every one of them, wore the ugliest expression they could manage.

※

The one who's left, the last one, maybe it's her? The one who declared on national television several years ago that there was no way in hell she would die until she heard those words? Those words had to come from a certain source and no other, not even God in Heaven.

She who had waited all her life to hear those words, it had to be Kunja. She who had kept her silence all those years until that day on television when suddenly she opened her blouse, declaring that she couldn't speak out unless she displayed her naked body for all to see.[6] And then she'd stripped off her undergarments and there it was, front and center on her belly, the scar that looked like a rusty zipper. "If they'd just removed my baby . . . then I could have had another one, I could have *lived*. But no, they cleaned me out, womb and all—how could they *do* that? And I never knew it—I tried to get pregnant, tried every fucking trick, I went to the temple, I prayed to the Buddha, I prayed to the three spirits, I *tried*, dammit, I even had a *mudang* do her song-and-dance!"[7]

When 16-year-old Kunja got pregnant and her belly began to swell, they said, "The bitch is young and pretty, low mileage on her, can't afford to trade her in yet, so just take out her uterus."[8]

More than sixty years ago she paid a visit to Kunja's home village. The two girls were the same age and she missed her terribly.[9]

North Kyŏngsang Province, Ch'ilgok County, Chich'ŏn Township . . . she kept repeating the address to herself. And there was her home at the end of an out-of-the-way sickle-shaped road, just as Kunja had told her. The barley in the fields was turning golden yellow on the stalk.

Even now she can picture the bean-sized birthmark beneath Kunja's mother's nose.

"And who are you, young lady?"

"I'm Kunja's friend."

Hearing this, the woman peppered her with questions. "Were you with her at the thread factory in Manchuria?"

When she didn't answer, the woman followed with, "Didn't she leave Manchuria?"

"You mean she's not here?"

"No! Didn't the two of you leave together?"

"No, we didn't." She didn't have the heart to tell the woman that they *had* left together but had gotten separated along the way.

"How come?"

"I wonder about that myself."

"How I wish the two of you had come back together!"[10] the woman wailed, and with tobacco-stained fingers grabbed her arm as if the arm itself were Kunja.

She was about to leave when the woman detained her saying she should eat first. Then she disappeared into the kitchen to stoke the firebox and make barley rice. Hearing that Kunja's friend from the thread factory was visiting, the other villagers dropped their work and rushed in from the fields.

A woman with missing teeth was the first to pounce. "Why didn't my daughter come back?"[11]

"Who is your daughter, ma'am?"

"Hŭisuk! Our Hŭisuk went with Kunja to the thread factory in Manchuria."

When she didn't respond, a villager wearing the dark, baggy pants that were standard attire for women in the countryside took her hand and asked, "How is our Sangsuk? Is she well?"

"Sangsuk?"

"Yes, Sangsuk. She has big round eyes."

"How come my daughter Myŏngok didn't come back?" another woman asked.

"I'm not sure . . ."

The neighbors left, distraught, and Kunja's mother asked her, "So you're the only one who came back?"

Am I the only one who survived?[12] She felt guilt clogging her throat so that the barley rice wouldn't go down.

Is it a sin if you're the only one who survives? Even if the place you survived is hell?

※

Glued to the window, she looks out at the alley. The diamond-pattern screen is rusting where the paint has peeled from it. A sliver of sunlight pricks her face.

Her gaze is fixed on the blotches of mold on the alley walls. A gust of breath explodes from her. *Seems like yesterday I heard forty-seven were left, but now it's only one?*

She retreats to the side, moving one foot then the other, over and over, like petals radiating from a flower. Each time she lifts a foot, air is sucked beneath the caramel-colored linoleum of the floor with its ugly punctures, scorch marks, warps, and scratches.

As if leaving behind a chapter of her life, she slowly turns away from the window.

No longer forty-seven.

What year was it, the year we lost nine, so that forty-seven were left? So before that . . . add nine to forty-seven. . . . But the simple math that works well enough when she's pricing items at the market or in the shops has broken down.

She fetches a bag of noodles from the kitchen and goes out to the veranda. It's a new bag, unopened, with which she can treat herself to a simple meal of noodles in broth. Perched on the edge of the veranda, she spreads a sheet of newspaper and empties the bag onto it. Picking up a noodle and setting it aside, she mumbles to herself, *one*; then repeats the sequence, *two*; then *three*; then *four*; ... and finally *fifty-six*. Add nine to forty-seven and there you have it.

She returns the noodles to the bag and is just about to step down from the veranda when she looks down at her feet and her face tenses. *Look at those dead magpies—what happened to her shoes! No, they're shoes, they're shoes, they're shoes*—but she just can't remove her gaze from her feet.

※

She takes a break from the dishes and sits down on the floor. Something is moving in her crotch, creaking like a loose, rusty nail.[13]

Poking with a nail was something else they did. Once when her overworked and swollen privates shut down, she was met with curses and the next she knew, they'd poked a nail inside her.[14]

※

She's taking a few light sweeps of the broom to the area surrounding the faucet when she catches sight of an army of ants swarming around a dead moth. How could a moth end up dead near the faucet? The next moment she's nodding. Dead moths could be anywhere—inside the wardrobe, in the sink, in the rice bin.

Sŏksun ŏnni—born in P'yŏngyang, South P'yŏngan Province, died in Manchuria. Before arriving at the comfort station in Manchuria, she'd worked at a tobacco factory packaging cut leaves of Long Life tobacco.[15]

"My shift lasted from eight to seven," she said, "and I earned enough money in a month to buy half a sack of rice."

"How'd you end up there?" said Hanok ŏnni; she sounded envious.

"I interviewed and had a physical. I'm small but I move fast and I have a lot of moxie, you know."

One day a year later Sŏksun ŏnni had returned home from the factory and was steaming kidney beans when a pair of constables came by. One rode horseback while the other was on foot. It was two days before the summer solstice and the evening was luminous. The walking man told her mother she had to send Sŏksun ŏnni to a textile mill in Japan.

"He had big, bulging eyes and he said they'd come and get me five days later and to make sure I stayed home that day. If I ran away, he'd have the whole family shot. What could I do? Mom was wailing—no way did she want to send me off. All I could think of was those kidney beans I was eating. They were *so* tasty. And sure enough, five days later they showed up in the middle of breakfast and off I went."[16]

"My time came when I was eating barley rice wrapped in lettuce," said Hanok ŏnni. "In comes Four-eyes with a stick up his ass and says we got to go *now* if we're going to catch the train. I couldn't even finish my meal. And here I am."[17]

"Who's Four-eyes?" said Tongsuk ŏnni.

"Kim, the local Jap stooge. Every dog in my home village knows Four-eyes."

Resting her broom against the veranda, she squats next to the moth.

The moth looks like a uterus. Her uterus, the army of ants sinking their tiny teeth into it and holding on for dear life reminding her of the line of Japanese soldiers jostling one another while awaiting their turn with her.[18] She begins to gag.

Clenching her fist, she extends her right foot and stomps down on the ants, sending them scattering in terror. Looking at the squashed ones upside-down, legs flailing, she removes her foot, shuddering at what she's done.

✺

She takes her sleeping pad from the wardrobe and spreads it on the floor beneath the mirror. Sitting with her back to the veranda, she passes her hand back and forth along the pad. The afternoon sun slants deep into the west-facing veranda. Her shadow on the pad fills out like spreading urine. Lying down on the pad, she looks up at the ceiling.

She closes her eyes but sleep doesn't come. No worries. She knows people can survive a lack of sleep.[19]

For seventy years now there hasn't been a single night that she's slept soundly. For when her body sleeps her soul is awake, and when her soul sleeps her body is awake.

She opens her eyes and turns slowly onto her side. She passes her hand along the sleeping pad once more, as if waiting for someone to lie down next to her. But no one comes.

2

HER SHOES ARE always there where she's put them. Always together, right shoe and left shoe, inseparable it would seem. The dusk settling over the shoes makes them look like a little girl's.

She's in her bedroom, sitting statue-like in front of the television. Sound carries from her room out to the veranda, but from there it would be difficult to tell if it's coming from the television or her lips.

The woman in the program is bent like a sickle blade. She's been cooking *pibimbap* for more than forty years at the same spot, she declares. Pork bones in a huge pot are being boiled down for soup stock. Next to the pot are a dozen bowls of vegetable-topped steamed rice ready to serve. The fresh soybean sprouts and strands of spinach and bracken fern cover every last grain of rice. The old stone masons are her regulars, the woman says.

The woman ladles enough boiling broth from the pot to scald the vegetables, then takes the bowl and returns the excess broth to the pot, carefully pressing the ladle against the rim of the bowl so no vegetables or rice escape. Steady and unspectacular, she repeats the process for half a dozen of the bowls.

The fingers of her left hand extend one at a time like the opening of a bud. A smile ripples across her face as she observes her open palm.

She often has visions of marsh snails squirming in the palm of her left hand. She imagines six of them in all—large, medium, and small—a nice little family of snails clustered in her palm.

Though she knows it's only an illusion, she frets that the snails will fall off. And sure enough one of the large ones begins to slide until it dangles precariously between her thumb and index finger. She retrieves it and back to the center of her palm it goes.

It's only a froth-like illusion but the wiggling sensation sets her trembling.

She knows that snails have an incredible life force. Worthless-looking creatures they may be, but they can hold out forever outside the water that sustains them.

It's been more than seventy years. Already . . .

It was more than seventy years ago, when she was gathering snails from the riverside marsh, that the men had appeared from out of nowhere and brought her up to the road. Where one man took her by the arms and another by the legs and she found herself being tossed into the back of a truck, suspended in air before crashing onto the floor of the cargo bin. Half a dozen other girls huddled there.[1]

She can't remember how many men there were—four or five?—only that they spoke Japanese among themselves. Their minder on the train from Taegu to Harbin was one of them.

Afraid they might kill her,[2] she dared not ask where they were taking her.

All she could think of was how scared she was.[3]

The truck stopped at an inn next to a stream and took on a group of girls. Far from being frightened like she was, they chattered away cheerfully, at one point cackling even. Before the truck left the inn she used the outhouse and on her way back spotted purple flowers on the hillside. While she gazed in wonder as if she'd never seen such flowers before, a girl approached. "Pretty, aren't they?"

"Yes. What are they called?"

"Bellflowers."

The girl was a head taller and wore a bell-shaped, knee-high black skirt with a long-sleeve, buttoned-up white blouse and *geta*.

"I can get you some?"

Without thinking, she nodded. As the tall girl headed up the slope for the flowers, one of the men yelled at her. Startled and flustered, the girl ended up trampling the flowers she was about to pick.

The crushed bellflowers remained stuck to the girl's *geta* all the way to Harbin.[4]

She was getting hungry by the time the truck arrived at the Taegu train station and let the girls out.

She's always regretted not trying to escape then and there, but even if she were to return to that time, she wouldn't dare think of making a run for it. The men who had taken her away kept an eye on the girls, and the station was crawling with Japanese military police and soldiers. Besides, she was overwhelmed by the magnitude of this station she had never seen before.

The girls clutched one another's hands to avoid being set adrift by the wave of humanity. Most of them were 15 or 16, and they sported every possible clothing style. One girl wore a Japanese cardigan along with the common baggy pants, and another girl was dressed in a white silk *chŏgori* and a black silk *ch'ima*.[5] She herself wore the funny-looking cropped pants[6] and the black *chŏgori* of coarse cotton that she had thrown on before going out to the marsh.

Dressed in a white *ch'ima* and *chŏgori*, her silky hair in a bun, holding to her chest a rooster in a wrapping cloth, an old woman stood not far from the girls, waiting for the train. The rooster stuck its head out through the wrapping cloth and jerked it left and right, showing its vivid crimson comb.

When the train's black snout came into sight far down the tracks, coughing up black plumes of smoke, her left hand formed a tight fist. Swept up in the flow, she and the other girls boarded the train, bound for God-knows-where. Her left hand held six snails, clutching them so tightly the shells dug into her palm.

Bringing up the rear as he herded the girls onto the train was a lanky, fiftyish man with a horse face. The one holding her by the legs when she'd been tossed into the back of the truck. Back then at least, a 50-year-old man was practically a grandpa.[7] His salt-and-pepper hair was unkempt and he wore a scruffy, oversize pair of pants beneath a white *chŏgori*. He turned out to be the man who distributed hardtack to the girls during the train trip.[8]

The compartment was flanked with pairs of seats that faced each other, each seat accommodating three girls. Pairs of Japanese soldiers paced the aisle.[9] The train had originated in P'ohang, and four girls from there were on board.

She could still feel the snails stirring in her hand when the train passed a place called Wŏnsan.

She tried to stay awake, afraid the snails would slip through her fingers and she'd never see them again. She clung to a hazy belief that the snails would return her to the riverside of her home. And so she kept moistening them with her fingertip lest they dry up and die. But the smelly-sweet spit she brought from her mouth to the snails dried in no time.

She's hit with a sudden thought: *How did she feel? When she heard the other woman had passed on and now she's the only one left?*

Frightened and lonely like a boat adrift on the vast ocean? Would it help if she knows I'm left too? Even though I'm not letting the world know, shouldn't I tell her I'm still here, that there's one more left?

But she has no idea where the last one is.

She herself was a comfort woman for the Japanese soldiers, but she's unknown to the world at large because she never went public and reported herself as such.

It occurs to her that there have to be others out there like her, former comfort women who out of shame or embarrassment have never gone public. What did they ever do wrong?[10]

Suddenly confused, she looks about her room, wondering where she is. Her eyes settle on the mirror.

Where could this be?

It's a question she must have asked herself hundreds of times during the train ride. *Where am I?* Until she got on the train in Taegu, the only world she knew lay within an hour's walk of her home.[11] She could vaguely tell the train was heading north.[12] North, ever north—but why? It was a question she couldn't voice.

So when the other girls mentioned "Taejŏn" she assumed they were in Taejŏn—and "Pongch'ŏn" meant Pongch'ŏn—and "Ch'ŏngjin," Ch'ŏngjin.[13]

She was all ears to the other girls' whispering.

"Are you going all the way to Manchuria?"[14]

"Yeah!"

"We are too!"

"I heard in Manchuria we can earn sackfuls of money."

To girls who had never strayed more than a few miles from home, Manchuria was "way up there."

"They told me I'll be a nurse,"[15] said a bucktooth girl in a red brocade chŏgori and a coal-black knee-high ch'ima.

"I'm going to work in a clothing factory," said a girl in a spring-green chŏgori with her hair in a long braid.

"I'll going to be weaving in a Yamada factory,"[16] said a pockmarked girl with narrow eyes.

"I'm going to a nice place!" said the girl from the Taegu station in the white silk chŏgori and black silk ch'ima. She had round eyes and flashed a grin.

"Did you say a nice place?"

"The ward-chief uncle promised he'd get me a job in a nice place . . . my father asked him what I'd be doing at this place and he just said it was a nice place, a nice factory—so anyway, all I have to do is go there."

"Do they pay well?"

"Depends on how I do . . ."[17]

"How about you?" she herself was asked by a girl next to her. "Which factory are you going to?" The wrist inside the girl's cotton sleeve looked so fragile.

"I'm not sure." She was about to follow up by saying she'd been taken away while she was out looking for snails, but then her gaze met the hardtack man's and she clamped her mouth shut.

Sometimes the train stopped awhile inside a tunnel.

Was it the third day or the fourth? She couldn't remember. They might have changed trains, but she had no distinct memory of that either.

When finally the hardtack man told the girls to get off the train, they'd arrived in Harbin. It was mid-May but felt like early March back home. The sky was cement gray and dreary. The girls didn't know it could snow up to their ankles there. Their unwashed faces, layered with days of smoke from the train, looked charred. The round-eyed girl's white *chŏgori* was sooty and wrinkled.

Everywhere you looked were swarms of Japanese soldiers. They were in constant motion, a blanket roll seeming to grow out of their back, a rifle slung over their left shoulder. Others were asleep on the bare ground, grimacing as if from nightmares, heads facing the same direction. A few had youthful faces and looked like boys who had fallen asleep after tiring themselves out romping around. One was grinding his teeth in his sleep. Not even a horse-drawn cartful of gravel passing close by could awaken them.

Off to the side of the station sat a mass of girls, each hugging a broadcloth bundle that was white or black. Their faces were dirty; maybe they hadn't washed for days either. She watched as a mud-caked truck with torn canvas over the cargo bin pulled to a stop in front of them.

For the better part of a day the truck bounced along a road across the wilderness plain before arriving at a building surrounded by a barbed-wire fence;[18] the structure had plywood walls and a tile roof.[19]

A dumpy woman in a light beige *kimono* came shuffling out in *geta*. As soon as she saw the girls emerging from the cargo bin, she started counting heads, like a rancher taking inventory of his livestock.

The sun was setting and the afterglow was blood red.[20]

Her gaze came to a stop at the far side of the barbed wire and she shrieked. A woman in a blue *kimono*, her face powdered with rouge, stood ghostlike; something was in her mouth. But it wasn't a woman after all, rather a scarecrow with a mouthful of *konyak* jelly.[21]

The woman counting the girls suddenly began squabbling in Japanese with the truck driver. Startled, she hid behind a girl with a bundle. The girl had clutched the bundle to her bosom all the while, but when the train passed Ch'ŏngjin she produced squares of rice cake from the bundle and shared them with the other girls. Her mother had packed them for her trip, she said. The snow-white rice cake was dotted with black beans the size of mouse eyes. The beans were turning bad, but the girls chewed them till there was nothing left.[22]

The driver, fuming by now, herded the girls inside the barbed wire. He had a mustache and wore a pair of sallow-colored knickers, a cheap fur cap, and gold-rimmed glasses with thick lenses.[23]

The woman instructed the girls to call her *haha*. *Haha* meant "mom" in Japanese, she learned later.

Haha told the girls they would have to take the soldiers beginning the next day. She herself understood this to mean they would cook their meals and wash their uniforms and socks.

"What do you mean, take the soldiers?"[24] said the girl who was supposed to be working at the Yamada factory. This girl didn't know whether the train was bound for China or Japan,[25] but was dead set on going to the Yamada factory. Hearing this, she herself figured the factory must be to the north.

"I mean you have to take the soldiers to bed with you,"[26] said *haha*.

Already puzzled at having arrived not at a factory but instead a hut-like structure resembling a pig pen, the girls now looked at one another, perplexed.

"Why would we take soldiers to bed with us?" The girl who issued this challenge was the one who during the train ride had pointed out to the other girls that they were passing through Kyŏngsŏng, P'yŏng-yang, Shinŭiju, and Antung and Changchun in Manchuria.

"This is a place where we take soldiers, so you have to take the soldiers."

"They told me I'd be a nurse—I didn't come here to take soldiers," said the girl with the buck teeth.

"We'll take good care of you if you sacrifice yourself for Imperial Japan."[27]

"They said they'd find me a nice place to work here," said the girl with the round eyes.

"That's news to me,"[28] said *haha* with a straight face.

"Why are you lying to us?"[29] said the girl who had shared her rice cake. Earning her a slap in the face from *haha*.

Whimpering and whining, another girl asked to be taken home. Not until she paid back all the money they'd spent to bring her here to Manchuria, said *haha*. No girl would go home until she paid off her debt.[30] She herself wanted to tell *haha* she'd been taken away while she was outside looking for snails, but she was too frightened to open her mouth.

"Think about it, girls—if you don't look after our brave soldiers, how can they win the war?"[31] said *haha*.

Another girl shook her head. "If I had known we'd be looking after soldiers, no way would I have come along." When she added that instead of taking soldiers she would cook and do laundry, *haha* slapped her too.

She herself still didn't understand what sleeping with soldiers meant, or sacrificing herself for Imperial Japan. Her only thought was that she missed her mom. When she broke into sobs and pleaded with *haha* to send her home she too was slapped. "Don't start!" snapped *haha*.

Haha then told the Yamada factory hopeful, "Starting today you're Fumiko." And that's how the pockmarked girl became Fumiko.

If *haha* said that starting that day a girl was Okada, then the girl became Okada.[32]

Night came and *haha* deposited each of the girls in a separate, box-like room.

※

When the girls were by themselves they called one another by the names they used back home.

She murmurs their names as they come to mind.

Kisuk *ŏnni*, Hanok *ŏnni*, Hunam *ŏnni*, Haegŭm . . . Kŭmbok *ŏnni*, Suok *ŏnni*, Punsŏn . . . Aesun, Tongsuk *ŏnni*, Yŏnsun, Pongae, Sŏksun *ŏnni* . . .
The girl sitting next to her on the train was Kisuk *ŏnni*.

Sundŏk, Hyangsuk, Myŏngsuk *ŏnni*, Kunja, Pokcha *ŏnni*, T'anshil, Changshil *ŏnni*, Yŏngsun, Miok *ŏnni* . . .

The girl on the train who said she was going to some nice place or other was Aesun, the one who was going to pick bellflowers for her was Tongsuk *ŏnni*, the girl bound for the Yamada factory was Pongae, and Hanok *ŏnni* had said she was going to work in a factory that made needles . . .

Yŏnsun said she had left home without telling anyone, not even her mother, pretending she was going to the outhouse and dressed as usual to avoid suspicion.[33] She was the oldest daughter and liked the idea of working at a factory and returning home with her earnings so her siblings wouldn't go hungry.

"When my mom had her youngest one it was tiny as a mouse, it was so malnourished," said Yŏnsun. "Grandmother told me that women who have babies but don't eat enough end up daft ... so I went house to house with a bowl, begging for food, and I managed to feed my mom."[34]

The girl who was convinced she'd be working as a nurse was Suok *ŏnni*.

Parched as pasteboard, the tongue inside her pursed mouth is twitching. A name lingers at its tip but doesn't quite come off.

She remembers all these names because she frequently recites them, like a child doing her multiplication tables. She'll count them off on her fingers as she calls them out, but still there are names that don't surface.

Some of the girls who were taken to Manchuria still went by a nickname; their parents hadn't yet come up with a name that would go in the family register.[35] One of these girls was from Pusan, and she had a heavy accent. At the comfort station this girl ended up with two Japanese names, one from *haha* and the other from a Japanese officer.

She herself was also given a Japanese name by *haha*. Which meant she had four names in all—her nickname at home, the name her father had made for the family register, that name mis-recorded in the register, and now the one from *haha*.

Add the names created by the soldiers and the total increased to a dozen. The soldiers who visited her body named her as they pleased.[36] Tomiko, Yoshiko, Chieko, Fuyuko, Emiko, Yaeko . . .

Maybe it was the one body and the four names that sometimes left her feeling that four different souls inhabited her.

Four souls in a five-foot-tall frame.

What she resented most in the comfort station was having only one body when dozens of men overran her like aphids.

That one body was not hers.

But she's made do with it and has survived until now.[37]

᪅

The day after their arrival, *haha* called the girls out to the yard. *Otosan*, her husband, who was also the truck driver with the cheap fur hat, herded them off across the plain.

Along the way they saw a Japanese army base. A roar broke out and there beyond a barbed-wire fence was a sprawling mural of soldiers in mustard-colored uniforms.

From there a thirty-minute walk brought them to a thatch-roofed structure coated with red dust;[38] it lacked the usual brushwood fence. A military truck was parked close by and Japanese soldiers hovered around. *Otosan* shouted at the girls to form a line. When the girls backpedaled, not wanting to be the first in line, he punched Kŭmbok ŏnni in the face. Startled, Kŭmbok ŏnni cupped her cheeks and returned to the front of the line. One by one the girls went inside. She herself was the third from the end. The twig door swung open and shut when the girls went in and out but she couldn't see inside.

Aesun was the first to go in, and when she came rushing out her face was ablaze as if she'd seen something she shouldn't have. Hitching up her black silk *ch'ima*, she rushed behind the truck and plopped down, looking for all the world as if she wanted to disappear. In the meantime Haegŭm went inside and soon after there was a scream. Kŭmbok was the third one in; she walked out with a nasty scowl. The shorter the line, the more frightened she herself became. She searched for a possible hideout, but *otosan*'s combat boots were trampling on her shadow.

Finally it was her turn. Waiting inside were a Japanese army doctor and a nurse. The nurse was a middle-aged Japanese woman with a large block of a face.

Speaking in a mixture of Japanese and Korean, the nurse had her step up onto a small wooden platform that looked like a chair with a square cut out from the seat. Mounting the platform, she realized why all the other girls had rushed out straightening their *ch'ima* in a fluster. They'd been brought here for a gynecology checkup and the platform was where they were examined.

"They brought us a baby. *Akachan-o thure-te kita-ne*," grumbled the doctor, a pale man, and then she saw the metal instrument shaped like a duck beak and felt it in her crotch.

Back at the comfort station *haha* handed out dirty-yellow sack dresses and showed the girls how to use *sakku*, condoms.

"Can't you send me home?" Aesun begged her.

"Don't worry. Just do as you're told and take a lot of soldiers, and then we'll send you home—you won't even have to ask."[39]

Haha unrolled a *sakku* over her thumb as a demonstration. It looked like a shriveled carp bladder.

That evening the girls began taking the soldiers. She was in the yard sobbing when she saw a group of Japanese soldiers surge toward the building. Next to her Haegŭm jumped up. Haegŭm, dejected from *haha* chopping off her hair as soon as the girls returned from their checkup, hair so precious not even her mother would have laid hands on it.

The laughing and banter of the aroused men turned boisterous. *Haha* shouted at the girls to go to their rooms.

The next morning she went to the canvas-covered laundry area in the backyard to find all the girls in tears as they washed their bloody underwear.[40]

The girls wouldn't make eye contact with one another. Her swollen privates made it difficult to close her legs as she squatted, urine dribbling from her with a burning sensation as if she'd been stung by a caterpillar.

"Let's kill ourselves,"[41] said Kŭmbok *ŏnni* to Tongsuk *ŏnni*.

Haegŭm's lower lip was bruised and swollen from where an officer arriving later in the night had bitten her. The swollen lip looked like a blood-gorged leech at rest.[42]

She can't remember how many men came and went that first night.[43]

They toyed with her all night long, a 13-year old girl, as if they were playing pick-up sticks.[44]

❋

She feels a spasm of shame. Flustered, she pounds her chest and mumbles to herself.

I've sinned so much . . .

She does this whenever and wherever—waking up in the middle of the night, crossing the street, waiting for the bus, having a meal— pounding her chest and mumbling these words. She's sinned so much, an unwary girl who knew nothing of the world a few miles beyond her home when she was taken away.

Though she'd done nothing wrong, she begged forgiveness from the Japanese officer who was the first of the men who visited her body. "I'm sorry, sir." With his bayonet the officer slashed her sack dress, leaving her feeling she had wings that were being slashed.[45]

While she was begging forgiveness, Kisuk *ŏnni* was begging for her life. And mercy be, Kisuk's soldier merely stabbed her in the thigh.[46]

In another room a petty officer struck a match to Haegŭm's pubic hair.[47]

The girls in this comfort station in Manchuria could hear one another's screams, an endless round of pain, through the thin plywood walls of their rooms. And they could hear one another moaning and groaning.[48]

3

THE ONE-STORY WESTERN-STYLE house she occupies is located in 15-*bŏnji*, the building and the plain cement-covered yard occupying barely fifteen *p'yŏng* of land. The faucet in the yard beside the outhouse sits in a housing just big enough for a washbasin.

Though it's her fifth year here, she's not the registered leaseholder—through no fault of her own she couldn't fill out the necessary change-of-address form. That's probably why from time to time she feels so fretful and uneasy there, as if she's sneaked into someone else's home.

There's a reason for all of this: the official leaseholders are her nephew's family in P'yŏngt'aek, and you can't report a new address if your name doesn't appear on the lease. The 15-*bŏnji* neighborhood is scheduled for redevelopment, and the residents have priority for lease-to-own rights to one of the new apartments that are going up. Knowing this, her nephew and his wife took out a lease on the house and filed the address-change form for themselves. In the mail she gets bills addressed to her nephew—for the residency tax and car insurance premiums, for example—as well as notices from the National

Health Service and the tax administration. This mail sits unopened in a neat pile until the next time he comes around.

The nephew is the son of her younger sister. She herself wasn't part of the family circle while he was growing up, which might be why he's never felt like a blood relation to her. And his blunt, offhand tendencies don't help. Which is why she felt both burdened and grateful when he offered her the house. She doesn't like accepting handouts, but when he practically got down on his knees and begged her, she gave in. Only then did he come clean about the priority right to the lease-to-own apartment and entreat her not to file the change-of-address when she moved in. That he was loath to register her as a resident was hurtful and upsetting, but she kept her feelings to herself. And she doesn't have to listen to the relatives jawing about a situation they're ignorant of to know what comes next: *What a nice guy he is to look after his poor, vagrant auntie when other people turn their backs on their own parents!*

And it's obvious to her why she of all people has been chosen by her nephew to occupy the leased house: she's childless,[1] which will present one less problem in the future.

People have no clue where she's been or to what she's been subjected.[2]

They can only assume that her marriageable years were spent drifting from one housemaid job to another. She never imposed on her family but could never bring herself to spill the truth even to her younger sisters, who considered her a burden and an eyesore: that she *hated* men; the mere sight of them made her shudder,[3] made her wish she had a gun with a silencer so she could exterminate them.[4]

Any talk of marrying her off sent her ballistic.[5]

Every month or two the nephew stops by. Supposedly he works security at an apartment complex. Her heart goes out to him. Just think, a man aged sixty-plus who's never owned a home of his own, who has to take out a lease in a condemned neighborhood to obtain priority rights to the new housing that's going up.

In the government registry she's listed as living in multi-unit housing in Hwasŏng, near Suwŏn. The landlady there must have a new renter by now. And good riddance to she herself: she once overheard the landlady lamenting to another tenant that before long she'd have a corpse on her hands.

Recently she happened to learn that a landlord has the right to file for nullification of a former tenant's official residency status if the tenant fails to submit the change-of-address form. She's afraid this has already happened—why, seven years later, would her landlady want to continue listing her as a tenant?

What's going to happen when the demolition starts? She wants to ask her nephew this but tells herself she shouldn't. It won't be long now, but still she takes the broom and the rag to the house morning and evening, paying special attention to the windows and doorways. The house is old, and if she slacks off in her cleaning, it shows.

※

She stops at the gate to look back at the one-bedroom house and finds herself wondering if a child was ever born there. Or—considering all the families who at one time in their lives had to live crammed together in a single room—if an extended family once lived there.

Every time she passes through the gate she feels she's leaving forever. Especially a few days earlier when she wasn't able to lock the gate on her way out, an experience that left her churning inside. It wasn't her fault, the lock was rusty, but still she felt as if she'd been driven from the house, and all she could do was squat miserably outside the gate.

The alley is thick with shadow and layered with a desolate silence. The house is the only one in the alley that's still occupied. You'd think that *someone* should be living in the two-story Western-style house at the far end of the alley, but it too is vacant.

In just two or three years there's been a drastic increase in the number of empty dwellings in 15-*bŏnji*. The only people remaining are, like her, those whose circumstances prevent them from leaving.

The alley gives onto another alley. This alley too is deathly still—it seems the last remaining occupants are gone.

For twenty minutes she wanders these alleys and not a person does she meet. Leaving her feeling that if she were to encounter someone, she'll want to give that person all of herself—her heart, liver, kidneys, even her eyes. But still she sees no one.

On her way down an alley that's steep as a slide she stops and looks intently at her feet.

She feels as if her feet are clad with dead magpies instead of shoes.

Even when she's convinced her shoes haven't turned to magpies, she can't remove her gaze from them. She's afraid that if she does, they will.

❖

The woman who does alterations is out. Her shop and the living space behind it add up to maybe three *p'yŏng* and are packed with what she needs to make her living: mother-of-pearl wardrobe trunk and dressing table, television, dining table for two, sewing machine, clothes-drying rack, chest with three drawers, electric fan. The dining table is strewn with pill bottles alongside a rice cooker. The drying rack is strung with handkerchiefs and underwear, and the floor beneath is littered with a glasses case, a roll of toilet tissue, cookie snack-packs, and such. This is where the woman eats, sleeps, and does finish work, attaching zippers to clothing and cords to curtaining.

Beneath the sewing machine is a lace-bedecked pink seat cushion with a white dog curled up on it. The dog is some 13 years old but small enough that you might mistake it for a puppy that's just been weaned.

The dog's been staring at her since she arrived, and now it makes an effort to rise but quickly curls up again. To her it seems more human than animal—probably the look. She marvels at how an animal is capable of producing a human look. Maybe it's only natural when an animal lives with a person, sharing the good times and the bad, the pleasure as well as the pain?

The dog's expression is so perfectly human it unsettles her. And its hair loss and the scabby eruptions on its skin are hideous.

She knows that over the years this dog has produced some fifty puppies. Every time its mistress gathers it in her arms and goes off on a spiel about its fecundity, she finds herself shaking her head. How could the little thing produce fifty puppies?

The woman has the dog artificially inseminated and sells the resulting litter at the pet market. The proceeds are nothing to sneeze at, the woman likes to say—after all it's a purebred and a preferred breed at the pet market. Whenever the dog is due, the woman anesthetizes it, makes an incision in its belly, and delivers the puppies herself before stitching the dog back up. That way she can account for every last one of the puppies. The dog's belly is an ugly belt of stitch marks, flesh abrading flesh.

She's about to leave but thinks better of it and eases herself down on the threshold. Reading her behavior, the dog comes down from the seat cushion, and the next thing she knows it's inching toward her, dragging its hind legs and rump. It settles close by, and now it's licking the hand that grips the threshold for support. It's a weird, tickling sensation and she closes her hand into a tight fist, but the dog takes no notice and licks for dear life.

She's discomfited by the devotion of this dog that's smaller than her foot, and at the same time feels sorry for it.

"Now stop that . . ."

She just can't understand it—the dog is practically basting her fingers with its tongue. Not once has she given the dog a good petting. It's nice the way it always welcomes her with a wag of its tail, but the way it mimics a human expression weighs heavily on her mind.

The alteration shop woman has returned. She watches her enter the shop but continues to let the dog lick her hand to its heart's content.

"The little darling, isn't she lovable," the woman says casually.

"She's a sweetie, all right," she says, her face betraying embarrassment as she pulls her hand back.

"Then maybe you'd like her for a pet?"

"Me?"

"She eats about as much as a bird, and she's long since potty-trained."

"But why . . . would you want to give her away?"

"I'd just as soon get rid of her if there's someone who wants her."

She knows that this woman doesn't sugarcoat her words, whether she's talking about herself or others, but doesn't beat around the bush either.

"You must be so attached to her, you've had her since she was a puppy—how could you give her to someone—"

"There comes a time when you have to let your kids go, why should it be any different with a dog?"

She's pretty much figured out the woman's scheme—now that the dog is too old to produce puppies, she wants to pass it on.

The woman's attitude toward the dog has thrown her into confusion. It's heartless the way the woman has the dog artificially inseminated whenever she wants it to turn out more puppies, but on the other hand she's terribly devoted to it—it's as if the dog is her own offspring. Just a few days ago the woman was for the longest time simmering a pollack head to feed it. She's not sure which of these approaches reflects how the woman really feels about the dog. Maybe they both do—but how could these different mind-sets, like the two poles of a magnet, coexist within the same person?

Was it forty years the woman said she'd been living in 15-*bŏnji*? She said she'd raised her three boys all by herself after her husband, a fireman, had died of cirrhosis of the liver. And when her boys were going through their growth spurt, she was up past midnight at her sewing machine, then up again by five in the morning to make two lunchboxes apiece for their long day of school and study. No way would she want to relive that period, the woman once declared, before adding that it was nevertheless a period worth living.

She finds her gaze wandering beneath the sewing machine. Before they've noticed, the dog is once again curled up on the seat cushion.

The woman goes to the refrigerator and returns with two glasses of milk, one of which she places in front of her. Seeing her merely staring at the milk, the woman picks up the glass and offers it to her.

"I'm sorry, milk doesn't agree with me . . ."

She just can't bring herself to say that it reminds her of semen.[6]

He told her to swallow his semen.[7] When she protested, the soldier unsheathed the knife from his waistband and stabbed the tatami.

The girls had to do what the soldiers told them. Soldiers had been known to shoot girls who didn't. Shoot them down below. As if they'd forgotten that where the muzzle was sighting in on was the very space where all of humanity had been fashioned.

One day a Japanese officer shot Myŏngsuk *ŏnni* down below. Because she'd refused, even after being beaten. Beaten unconscious, she continued to refuse after she came to. The bullet passed through her uterus. It didn't kill her, but it left her like a rotten pumpkin down there.[8]

Eating shit would be better than this. She grimaced as she swallowed the fluid.[9]

And she can't eat squid. Because the suction cups remind her of the mounded sores that erupted in her groin when she came down with syphilis. When the sores erupted even her eyes would start itching. *Itching so badly she felt like poking her eyes with a needle.*[10]

Back out in the alley she wanders around.

"Why me?" she murmurs.

She thinks she knows why the woman's attitude toward the dog is beyond confusing, is painful to her even. It reminds her of *haha*, the woman who ran the comfort station.

Haha gave the girls Japanese names and provided them with food and clothing. She also distributed *jimigami*—coarse, dark-colored toilet tissue[11]—as well as olive green soap, toothbrushes, tooth powder, gauze menstrual pads, and towels. And a navy blue sleeveless dress that looked like a rice sack.

When the girls didn't pay attention, *haha* would tell on them to her truck driver husband, the man who had delivered them from the Harbin train station. He had been in the army, and the girls called him *otosan*—which, she had learned from Kŭmbok *ŏnni*, was Japanese for "father." On the wall of the kitchen, where the girls took their meals, was a photo of *otosan* in a military uniform sporting two dots that you might almost take for stars.[12] While the girls sat around the plywood dining table taking their meal, *haha* and her family ate among themselves. The girls took in the aromas of pike mackerel and beef soup. Those items didn't appear on their table, which bore only watery gruel and pickled radish.

Haha and her family lived in a hut apart from the comfort station. *Otosan* spent his days in a room near the entrance to the station where, armed with sword and pistol, he kept watch over the girls. To keep them from escaping, he had strung electric wire around the compound.

When she thinks of *haha*'s two daughters a strange thought occurs to her: those little girls also referred to *haha* as *haha*.

Come to think of it, the alteration shop woman had also tried to hand off her dog to the woman who runs the Seoul Beauty Parlor. This woman had flat out said no; she was born in the year of the tiger and the poor dog would be scared shitless in her presence. The beauty parlor woman is the sort who believes that marriage compatibility is a matter of fate, and she understood her husband's vagabond nature—he was an itinerant construction worker—as an inevitable result of their conflicting personalities, which made it necessary for them to live apart from each other if their marriage was to survive. She herself found it dubious that a husband and wife doomed with combative personalities were so strongly attracted to each other that they could marry and have two children. If they were in fact bad news for each other, shouldn't they have cut their losses and run off in opposite directions before they tied the knot?

She doesn't know if the determination of a person's fate is a matter of the alignment of the stars, temperament, or the will of the gods. Perhaps it's a combination of all three?

She's not sure if the gods exist, but there are times she feels them. When she sees the first light of dawn through the milky glass of her window, when a flock of sparrows take flight from the woods, when she bites into a sweet, juicy peach. . . . Now that she's figured out it's the gods she senses, she's surprised at how often she's felt them at work. The first time she saw bellflowers she felt the gods.

And at the same time she feels fright.

And even though she's not sure the gods exist, you won't find her picking up fruit that's fallen from someone else's tree, for fear that one of the gods might see her. And you won't hear her curse another, even in an undertone, for fear a god might hear. Indeed, she thinks that perhaps she's more afraid of the gods than the people who trust in their existence.

But the real reason she's turned down the woman's offer of her dog is this: what if she breathes her last before the dog lives out its days?

People are always urging her to keep a dog or a cat; after all, she doesn't have a husband or children. The elderly woman who took her in as a housekeeper for six years went so far as to say she had the heart of a person who could revive any living thing. This after seeing her minister to houseplants that had shriveled and seemingly died at the hands of the daughter-in-law but now, miracle of miracles, were blooming anew! This gift was enough, said the mistress, to revive a person on death's doorstep. She herself, though, believed that her revival of the houseplants resulted not from her green thumb but from always going the extra mile. Her success with the plants owed to feeding them with water used for rinsing the rice, finding the sunniest place to put them, and watching morning, noon, and night for any sign of withering.

Even if she was convinced that at age 93 she would outlive the dog, she would refuse it anyway. For she's not sure she can prevent a pet from getting sick and dying.

She does have Nabi, who likes to hunt and then bring her the trophies. And as much as she wishes Nabi wouldn't do that, her greater hope is that one day the cat won't return from its hunting expedition. At the same time, if it's gone even four days she feels anxious. She wonders how old the cat is. And if it ever had another master. And if so, if that person abandoned it.

She's afraid that someday Nabi will bring home a live magpie and drop it at her feet.

And the next time a dead girl.

⁂

The comfort station in Manchuria was a living hell. Even if you wanted to hang yourself, there wasn't a single tree fit for the purpose. Out on the plains there were only scrub oaks and a scattering of husk-like shrubs poking out of the ground. You had to go high up in the hills to find trees worthy of the name. Four long days of scrambling across the highest of the high hills would get you to Soviet land.

And so the girls would cut themselves and bleed to death while high on opium. Knowing that if they cut a finger and sucked long enough to get the blood flowing, the opium would put them to sleep and they'd never wake up.[13] Kisuk ŏnni had died like that, her blood-caked teeth looking like pomegranate kernels.

Back in her ancestral home of Miryang, Kisuk ŏnni had worked at a cotton-gin operation run by the Japanese. You put the cotton bolls from the field into the gin, and it separated the cotton from the seeds.

Kisuk ŏnni said she had seen a man get dragged into the machine by his hair.[14]

"He was a distant relative," Kisuk ŏnni had said, "and his daughter saw it too. What could any of us do except jump up and down and scream. . . . She was the same age as me, and she didn't have a proper name and so we called her Monnani, the ugly one. Monnani went off before I did. After what happened to her father, she was the only one in the family who could bring money in. . . . She said she was going to work in a munitions factory in Japan. . . . I can still visualize that accident, it was so real, so imagine what it was like for her. It was the hair that got caught . . . just a few strands of it . . . and as soon as we said *uh-oh* his head was sucked in . . ."

The morning Kisuk ŏnni died she got an injection of opium from *otosan* and went out to the yard and started dancing. She pulled at the sleeve of the *kimono* the scarecrow was wearing, so that it looked like she was dancing along with the scarecrow. *Haha* called this scarecrow Haruka. Haruka's face was redder than it was the day the girls arrived at the comfort station. Supposedly *haha* daubed it with blood every night. None of the girls saw her doing this, but Haruka's face got redder by the day. Unlike the faces of the girls, which turned a sickly yellow or black.

After what happened to Kisuk ŏnni, she dreamed she was slinking down the hallway of the comfort station. Calling to Kisuk ŏnni, telling her it was time for breakfast. *Haha* provided only two meals a day, so if you missed breakfast you either went hungry all day or got by on hardtack from the soldiers. The girls often missed breakfast when officers arrived late at night.[15] In her dream she just couldn't find Kisuk ŏnni's room—the names of the girls had all been removed from the doors.

Haha had made name tags for the girls and posted them on the doors. Umeko, Kiyoko, Fumiko, Eiko, Kinoe, Asako. . . . The girls who came down with gonorrhea or syphilis had their name tags turned inside out, and the soldiers didn't line up outside their doors.

The name tags were made of wood and were hung lengthwise. They were about the size of a container for spoons and chopsticks and resembled a memorial plaque bearing the name of the deceased, which made her feel as if the names written on them were those of the girls who had died rather than the ones still alive.

Haha didn't bother burying Kisuk *ŏnni*. Why waste dirt and soil on her?[16]

The girls had been told they'd be issued new rubber footwear and be fed full portions of rice, not the chaffy stuff.[17] They had no idea that the place they went to upon hearing these promises was a living hell.

And in this living hell the girls were flogged with *soekkudae*,[18] whips with metal handles; beaten with red-hot fire pokers[19] or with metal bars;[20] hit with the flat of a sword; or kicked indiscriminately.[21] *And they stuck red-hot metal rods into the girls' vaginas. The rods came out with charred flesh stuck to them.*[22]

❋

She's in an alley where no one lives. She stops and looks at all the empty dwellings. They're of every size and shape imaginable. One moment she'll see a house shut tight, windows and all, the next moment a house with its gate open wide onto the alley. There are houses with shattered windows, the shards of glass strewn in the alley, and houses with overflowing piles of trash and abandoned furniture.

If it was her, she'd want to make sure she'd shut all the doors and windows before vacating.

Some places it's hard to tell whether they're vacant or inhabited. Somehow the house she occupies strikes her the same way.

She worries about the empty houses in 15-*bŏnji*, thinking of them as birds and hoping they'll fly off before the wrecking crews and the excavators arrive.

There were houses on the Manchurian plains. They come hazily to mind now, dwellings appearing in the distance from the cargo truck that picked them up in Harbin. Houses made of boards slapped together, houses with brushwood fences, sooty structures that looked more like fireboxes than homes. Houses resembling migratory birds taking a respite from their endless journey to feed on bugs and stray grain.

When the plains became bare, with neither house nor tree in sight, Haegŭm mumbled anxiously, "I wonder how far it is to the silk factory."

The truck was rattling terribly, but her face and eyes showed that Haegŭm herself was rattled. *We were too young, we didn't know a thing;* they never doubted[23] how it came to be that they were all led to believe they were going to different factories. She herself didn't care if it was a factory that made thread, silk, or needles; if it was a good or a bad place to work; she just wished they would get there.

There were in fact girls who had gone to factories to make money. Miok *ŏnni* had left school in the sixth grade at the urging of her principal and joined the Workers Service Corps. She took the streetcar to Kyŏngsŏng Station and with other girls boarded a train for Pusan. Young as she was, she thought only that she was off on a trip to some distant place.[24] At Pusan she boarded a shuttle ferry named *Kamome*, which means "seagull," to Shimonoseki, where she was loaded onto a truck and taken to a munitions factory in Toyama Prefecture that made cartridges for assault rifles. Her work table was so high she had to stand on a chest to do her work. One area of the factory was stacked with brassware confiscated from Korea to be melted down and made into weaponry. Not once was Miok ŏnni compensated during the time she worked at this factory.[25]

At the comfort station Kisuk ŏnni, hearing that Miok ŏnni had been at a munitions factory in Japan, asked, "You must know Monnani, then?"

"Monnani?"

"Well, Monnani said she was going to work at a munitions factory."

"There wasn't anyone named Monnani where I worked."

"That's strange . . ."

When Kisuk ŏnni cocked her head dubiously, Miok ŏnni followed up with, "Where was this Monnani from?"

"Miryang."

"We had a lot of girls from Chinju and Masan but none that I know of from Miryang."

"At the factory where I worked," said Ch'unhŭi ŏnni, "there were a lot of girls from Chŏlla."

Ch'unhŭi ŏnni had worked at a clothing factory. From eight in the morning to seven in the evening she did laundry, cleaned up, and made clothes. At that factory were women in their thirties who had left their children back in the home village so they could go out to make money.

"The dinner they fed us was so measly you could practically count the grains of rice. And until dinner all they gave us was three lumps of rice cake that was more like bean cake. I used to wrap it in cloth and stick it in my waistband, then eat it later by myself—along with all the lice that lived there, no doubt. Before I got here I sent a telegram home asking my family to send me salt and beans . . ."

After several months at the clothing factory some fifteen of the girls were summoned, put on a truck, and taken away. They ended up in a large room. Japanese soldiers arrived and the girls found themselves being taken one at a time to smaller rooms. After that the girls, but only the younger ones, were scheduled by the day—on Tuesday the Tuesday girls went out to the smaller rooms, on Wednesday the Wednesday girls went out, and so on.

The days the girls didn't have to go out to serve the soldiers were days of freedom.[26]

"This MP asked me how old I was," said Ch'unhŭi ŏnni. "I guess because my face is kind of round like a baby's . . . anyway I told him I was 13, and he went 'Wow' and laughed."

Ch'unhŭi ŏnni was 15 when she arrived at the Manchuria comfort station. Her round baby face, as she called it, became sunken and pointed like a trowel. From her very first day she was desperate to escape. She made a nuisance of herself playing sick to *haha*, anything to reduce the quota of soldiers she had to take. The other girls went about with mouths pursed like goldfish, going through the motions even when singing "Kimigayo," the Japanese national anthem, and reciting the Rescript for Loyal Citizens.

Before breakfast the girls gathered on the lawn outside the comfort station. Standing immobile facing the Japanese flag, with loud voices they sang the anthem and recited the rescript.

It was summer and from early in the morning the air reeked of the outhouses. The girls staggered out onto the lawn with dazed expressions, as if addled by nightmares, and stood watching the flag. The sunlight landing on the nape of Haegŭm's neck felt prickly. She stood somnolent, her head down. Blowflies just hatched in the outhouses buzzed among the girls. All summer long the outhouses spawned maggots, mosquitoes, and blowflies. Ch'unhŭi ŏnni was scratching her face, which was patchy from malnourishment, and half mumbling, half cursing. Hanok *ŏnni* was grabbing at her armpits. The lice were a constant presence and had found a home there as well.

She moved next to Yŏnsun. "What happened?"

In the wee hours of the morning she had heard Yŏnsun scream. And then a door being kicked in. Feet running down the hall. *Otosan* and a soldier tussling. It had gone on for quite some time.

Thousands of years of happy reign be thine;
Rule on, my lord, till what are pebbles now
By age united to mighty rocks shall grow
Whose venerable sides the moss doth line.

The girls started singing, and she and Yŏnsun joined in. Suddenly Yŏnsun plopped down, yellowish pus streaming from between her thighs. A blowfly came to rest on her open, blackened mouth.

Even as the girls sang in praise of the emperor and pledged their undying loyalty as citizens of the empire, the lice were feeding on their blood.

Today the memories of the comfort station in Manchuria are especially vivid. The building had block walls overlaid with plywood and was filled with rooms flanking the bamboo-straight hallways. The slipshod wooden floors of the hallways creaked loudly day and night. At the end of one of the hallways was the kitchen; it had a dirt floor and a Chinese-style firebox for cooking. Atop one of the board shelves the girls' rice bowls were stacked like a tower, round bowls made of nickel. When the rats were active *haha* put out pieces of cardboard bearing a glue-like substance. *Haha* didn't like people coming and going from the kitchen, and the only time the girls were allowed in was when they came for water. Whenever she went to the kitchen for water and saw the rats stuck fast by their feet or tail to the cardboard, she felt a close kinship with them. Once she found a couple of baby rats stuck to the cardboard; the mother rat was looking on, fire in her eyes.

The yard in front of the comfort station was bare earth except for a few clumps of tangled grass. A stream went past the yard out back. A channel had been carved for the stream, and where the water pooled, an area for washing up had been curtained off with thick sheets the color of military fatigues. Fed by the stream water, half a dozen lengths of hose resembling fat worms stuck out of the ground, each one topped by a ladle-like showerhead.[27]

The three plywood outhouses had locks made of a yellow metal. *Haha* gave the keys to the girls, in effect making the outhouses off-limits to the soldiers. Otherwise the pits would be overloaded in no time and stink to high heaven. The only time the girls gave out the keys was to the officers who arrived at night.[28]

Each of the girls' rooms had an opening set ridiculously high in the wall. What's more, the window was curtained with a thick cotton drape that fell nearly to the floor, so even during daytime the rooms were dark as caves.

On average the rooms were about one and half *p'yŏng* in area. There were rooms slightly smaller and rooms slightly larger. When new girls arrived at the comfort station, *haha* would hang a blanket in the larger rooms, partitioning them in two.

When she sees the upper windows of the buildings bordering the alleys she can't help but relate them to the windows in the rooms of the comfort station. Even the tallest girls were barely head-high to the windowsill.

✳

There she is again.

She recalls the first time she encountered this girl. She saw her approaching from the far end of the alley and startled. *Punsŏn, back from the dead!* With her cropped hair and eyes as round as a bird's, the girl definitely resembled Punsŏn.

Punsŏn, taken from the cotton fields where she worked. Punsŏn, calling out *It hurts, it hurts,*[29] every waking moment at the comfort station.

When Punsŏn's infection down below made it difficult for her to walk, *haha* cut into the pus-filled flesh with her dagger. After squeezing out the pus she stuck a cotton ball coated with a white powder to the area.

There was a Japanese officer, ready for action, who said to Punsŏn, "Let's have some fun." But she didn't understand Japanese and just stood there. Whereupon the officer grabbed her and threw her to the ground.

The girl is wearing a backpack and squatting at the base of the wall, next to a crack that looks like a slash mark. She hasn't seen her for a few months and assumed the girl had moved.

It's a miracle the girl is still here in 15-*bŏnji*. There are precious few children left. When she moved in she could hear children's voices from time to time, but by now practically all the families with children have moved. Growing up in 15-*bŏnji* has become bleak and anarchic. Maybe that's why this girl strikes her as the one girl left not only in 15-*bŏnji* but in the whole world.

Today as always the girl is by herself. She's never seen the girl with friends.

The girl wears a small yellow dress that stretches tightly across her chest and leaves her thighs exposed. Because she's squatting, the hem of her dress is rolled up to her hips, and her panties are in and out of view. Maybe the girl doesn't have a mother? Or maybe the mother is off to work and leaves the girl to her own devices? If she were the girl's mom she wouldn't be letting her wander the alleys of 15-*bŏnji*. The girl doesn't look like she's beyond the age where she'd be playing the baby with her mom, but there's definitely something more girlish than baby-like about her.

With half a mind to pull the girl's dress down, she approaches gingerly. And yet the girl is already on guard and the next moment the vigilance has changed to hostility.

Stopping to read the girl's intentions, she catches sight of an object resting in the hand that lies limp against the pavement. Her mouth widens as she gawks at it.

"A mask—something you made at school?"

Not a wooden mask but a mask made of paper pulp. Examining the mask, she cocks her head inquisitively. The mask has eyes and a nose but no mouth.

The girl gets up and sticks out the mask toward her. "Try it on."

She flinches at the girl's voice, which to her ears is obnoxiously loud.

"Try it on," says the girl, fretful now.

Don't tell me she made that mask just for me?

It's not a huge request, but she doesn't feel right about it. There's no mouth, the entire surface is purple, it gives her the creeps.

It's only a mask made of paper pulp but somehow she feels it would stick to her face and she wouldn't be able to get it off. She doesn't know how many days she has left in this world, but she would have to live out those days with this mask stuck to her face. And even when she's dead and buried and her face has rotted away, the mask would remain intact, wandering underground.

"I told you to try it on!" Now it's an order.

She knows she can't win and takes the mask.

A sly, mischievous expression comes over the girl's face, which is oddly contorted. But the next instant it looks old and weary, as if the girl has experienced every conflict life can throw at her.

She tries to avoid looking at the girl's face as she observes the mask she's holding. It has a garish shine from its coating of paint and varnish. The gleam gives the mask a peculiar expression that she who is human cannot mimic.

Only after inspecting the alley to make sure no one is watching the two of them does she bring the mask to her face. She positions it this way and that so her eyes can see through the holes, then realizes the holes and her eyes are not equidistant and the mask won't fit. One eye might but then the other one won't.

Before she's finished she hears the girl's shrill laughter. Then it seems to grow distant, and suddenly it's gone. Only then does she remove the mask and look about the alley; the girl is nowhere to be seen.

"Hey, sweetie, you need to take your mask . . ."

Her fear-ridden voice rings hollow in the alley.

Is the mask a gift? A gift of the gods, sent by way of the girl? The mask using the girl as a medium, like the dead magpie used the cat as a medium?

She finds the mask more terrifying than the magpie. She can't return dead magpies whence they came, but she would like to return the mask.

But she doesn't know where the girl lives. Once she secretly followed the girl in an attempt to find out. It was a game of hide and seek, the girl leading her on a circuitous trip through the alleys, only to vanish in the blink of an eye.

How old could the girl be—10? 11? 12? 13? Every time she goes out the gate of the house she occupies, she decides that if she sees the girl in the alleys she'll ask—but she always forgets.

The girl couldn't have reached age 13 yet. She still can't believe that's how old she herself was when she was taken away back then.

One night at the comfort station a drunken officer took his dagger and made a cut in her privates. She was barely 13 and her underdeveloped genitalia wouldn't admit him.[30]

Could the last one be Aesun? Aesun with her swarthy face and thin eyelids drank the potassium permanganate solution she was supposed to dilute with water to clean her privates. Fortunately Kŭmbok ŏnni found her and made her throw up. But the solution left her throat raw.[31] And her vocal cords too, so that she sounded like a parrot when she spoke.

The tiniest drop of this solution turned water red, a little more made it black. Fatal if swallowed, it was used for washing the girls' privates.[32]

˟

Wandering in search of the girl in the yellow dress, she finds herself in front of the mini-mart. The man who runs it is combing his wife's hair. Eyes closed, the wife entrusts herself to him, and it's like he's taken her in his embrace the way he supports her from behind. Even at a distance she can almost feel the trembling hand holding the orange, hatchet-shaped comb. *How marvelous—he's got the palsy and there he is combing her hair!* Combing as if it's the only task left for him in this world.

The wife is paralyzed from the waist down and keeps to the living quarters at the back of the shop, lying sideways and facing out. From there she does checkout for the customers and their purchases. The alteration shop woman finds her unsightly and won't buy so much as a pack of gum there. Even though she knows the mart woman would have an awful time hoisting herself to a sitting position.

Maybe they're having the time of their life, this couple. Maybe it's so they can savor this blessing for as long as possible that he takes the longest time combing her hair.

As far as she knows, he used to work at city hall, was the envy of all, but gambled away a fortune and the family was ruined. To pay off his gambling debts he went to work at a fish farm on a coastal island and there he had a stroke. The alteration woman blames the wife's disability on the husband. *I mean, think about it,* she'll say. After the husband had his stroke, the wife did this, that, and the other thing to pay off what remained of his debt, and then one day she slipped on a sheet of ice and injured her spinal cord. Three surgeries later she still couldn't stand, and that's when the man took on the mini-mart.

There, he did it, he's dropped the comb. Standing still as a statue, she waits for him to pick it up.

※

Her feet have brought her to an alley she doesn't normally visit; 15-*bŏnji* is a labyrinth of interlocking alleys with no apparent logic to the layout. Some of the alleys seem endless, others are short and blunted, and just when you're getting used to them forking in two or even three, you run into a dead end. And then there are the alleys that look like roller coasters.

And now guess what? It's the old man. Who's never by himself, who always has his son in tow. The son is well over 50 but functions at the level of a 5- or 6-year-old due to a birth defect. You would never believe the two of them are father and son. The father with his knotty chin and wavy hair is slight and appears to be bending over to get a closer look at the world, whereas the son is gigantic like a wrestler, his eyebrows thick and his features well defined.

She's often witnessed the father cajoling the massive son after he's stopped dead in his tracks in the alley. But she's never seen him snarling and threatening the son or venting his fury at him.

According to the Seoul Beauty Parlor woman, the old man is absolutely devoted to the son. Decades ago he was visited by social workers who suggested sending the son to a facility; the old man grabbed a kitchen knife and all hell broke loose. Since then no one has dared bring up the issue with him.

What if I run into them? This is her constant concern, even though it's this father and son whom she encounters most frequently among the denizens of 15-*bŏnji*. They've never once acknowledged her, much less harassed her, but her heart goes into overdrive at the sight of them.

She's hit by a urine stink but can't tell if it's coming from them or from the alley.

The old man roams 15-*bŏnji* scavenging electric wire from the deserted homes, then strips out the copper and sells it to the junk dealer. The old man's house is down the hill from the house where she lives, separated by two alleys, its backyard visible beyond the collapsed wall. The yard is a war zone of bundles of electric wire and copper.

She wonders how he strips the copper from the wire. *Like peeling blood vessels from a dead animal?*

Oh no! There it is, the orange onion sack. And inside it a kitten.

It's the old man's side job. He's a merciless hunter of kittens in 15-*bŏnji*, and he sells them at the market. No one raises a stink about it—the kittens are strays bred among strays. According to the beauty parlor woman he gets 5,000 *wŏn* per kitten—at the very least.

Four months ago she was roaming the alleys like today when she came across the old man at work: his hand shaped like a bird's foot darting out to grab a kitten around the neck, then stuffing it into the orange onion bag as the terrified creature clawed at the air, then hanging the elongated bag from the gate of the nearest of the vacated houses. The ideal snare, that mesh bag.

All the while, the adult son looked on meekly like a grade schooler in detention. She feels somehow as if the entire process is being imprinted step by step on his brain.

This time the old man hangs the bag with the kitten from a utility pole and strides off down the alley.

Whether from exhaustion or resignation the kitten in the bag is dead still, not thrashing about, not yowling. On the one hand it would seem fortunate if the kitten has early on accepted its fate, but at the same time she's nagged by a thought: judging from the bones jutting against its hide, it wasn't nursed much.

If 15-*bŏnji* were a backwoods hollow instead of a redevelopment zone where cats run free, would the old man be hunting rabbits, pheasants, or boar?

She also wonders what he'll buy with the 5,000 *wŏn* he gets for a kitten? Rice, eggs, salt, *ramyŏn*, milk, potatoes, flour?

At the mini-mart 5,000 *wŏn* will buy a tray of eggs. About a month ago she saw him purchase a tray of eggs there.

Or maybe he uses that money to pay for his electricity, his water, his gas?

Sensing her presence, the kitten releases a feeble but persistent meow. Her face hardens as she looks about the alley. No one there but her and the kitten.

The bag is within reach if she gets up on tiptoe. But she dares not retrieve the bag and free the kitten. She no longer has the heart.

It's not that she lacks mercy but rather she's too old to be dispensing it. This is how she rationalizes it, but still she's swept by guilt. She tries to convince herself that no harm's been done, and yet she feels something wicked has happened.

As soon as the kitten was bagged it belonged to the old man.

Just like the girls became the property of a *haha, okusan, obasan,* or *otosan* after they were snatched and taken away while weeding the field,[33] picking cotton,[34] fetching water from the village well,[35] returning home from washing laundry in the stream,[36] heading to school,[37] or tending to their ailing father.[38]

Back in the beginning, was that how people staked out the virgin land? And the chestnut trees, the persimmon trees, and the other trees that bear nuts and fruit? And the streams? And the dogs, the goats, the pigs, and the other pets and livestock?

At the Manchuria comfort station the girls were livestock, no different from chickens or goats. If the girls didn't obey or were caught trying to escape, *otosan* would lead them around by a leather leash looped about their necks.[39]

4

SHE STANDS OUTSIDE the gate, gaze fixed on the house. She feels she's been gone since she was a baby [1] and is allowed to return only now that she's aged all she possibly can, almost a century later.

She's scared to open the gate and enter the yard. She'd like to return to the alley but realizes she has no place to go. [2]

※

Placing the mask from the girl off to the side of the veranda, she goes to the faucet, turns it on, and watches the water gurgle from the sky-blue hose. As the water swirls around the drain she has the illusion she's being swept away by it.

She stares blankly as the reflection of her face in the washbasin breaks up, then tilts the basin to empty the water as well as the reflection, the water reminding her of the tap water with which she used to clean her privates at the comfort station.

Haha instructed the girls to use a solution, but she preferred plain water because the red color of the solution made her feel she was washing her privates with the blood of a farm animal.

The number of times she washed herself equaled the number of men who had come and gone from her the previous day. She washed and she washed until the flesh she washed felt as if it belonged to someone else and not her. Having to use cold water even in winter, she could feel the cold invade her down below.

Pretty, oval-faced Hyangsuk, a P'yŏngyang *kisaeng* academy graduate who was coveted among the officers, suffered terribly from menstrual cramps. Unable to take men during her period, she was led to the nearby village by *haha*, who instructed a Chinese gynecologist to apply an icepack to her privates. It felt like her frozen privates were breaking off, she whimpered, and then out squirted a flood of dark blood.[3]

"Your blood's dead!" declared Kŭmbok *ŏnni*.

Word got out among the girls that the icepack treatment had shrunk Hyangsuk's uterus to the size of a chicken gizzard.[4]

Haha and *otosan* would have a girl's uterus removed at their pleasure—yet another way in which the girls were treated like livestock. If a girl got pregnant, her uterus was removed fetus and all as a preventive measure. A pregnant girl wouldn't fetch the price of a dog.[5]

Barely 13 when taken to the comfort station and with no experience of a menstrual cycle, she saw how hot and bothered the mature girls were about the possibility of becoming pregnant. If a girl showed signs of morning sickness or a bulging stomach, *otosan* took her away in the truck, and by the end of the day the girl would return looking as if she'd been drained of blood.

The girls simply couldn't imagine their uteruses being cut out.

Even with all the on-the-spot abortions and uterus removals, there were a few girls who got pregnant and had a baby, thanks to a torn or unused *sakku*.

When she missed her period, Ch'unhŭi *ŏnni* had a pregnancy scare and tried to induce an abortion with a clothes iron. Hanok *ŏnni* handled the iron, using chopsticks to feed its fuel box. The more coals she added, the hotter the iron became.

Ch'unhŭi *ŏnni* scowled. "Damn, that's *hot!* Are you sure this gets rid of it?"

"Just keep still!" barked Hanok *ŏnni* as she added one more coal.

Hanok *ŏnni* also knew that granny-flower roots would do the job. They bloomed all around the family burial mounds back home. She kept her eyes peeled for them in Manchuria but no luck.[6]

From the time she starting having a period she was scared above all else by the tearing of a *sakku*, afraid she would catch a disease or get pregnant. Any semblance of a tear and she would bolt up and beg the irritated soldier to use a new one.[7]

When she bolted up as if thunderstruck, fleas shot from her like sesame seeds in a fry pan.

Haha also handed out bean-sized pills. Supposedly they prevented disease. Once when she thought no one was looking she threw hers into the outhouse pit, but *haha* found out and she caught a beating. *I had to go and tell her I threw them away—why didn't I just say I took them?* She didn't know how to lie.[8]

The strong-smelling pills felt like fire in their nostrils. The girls had no idea they were made of mercury.[9]

Even during their periods the girls took the soldiers. Deep into their vagina went a cotton ball the size of a quail egg to block the flow of blood. The more soldiers they took, the deeper the cotton ball went.[10] Whenever she spread her legs to put in the cotton, she felt downy like a duck.

Very rarely there would be a stillbirth. Too much scrubbing with the solution and the injections of the toxic 606 tended to make sure a fetus wouldn't survive till birth.[11]

Once while they were eating, Suok *ŏnni* began writhing in pain. Kŭmbok *ŏnni* felt her belly. "I think you're pregnant."

Suok *ŏnni*'s face turned white.

A few days later *otosan* took her in his truck to the nearby village. What with the soldiers they were taking, the girls didn't notice Suok *ŏnni*'s return until the next morning. Peeping into her room, they saw her shivering and heard her teeth chattering. The blanket that covered her body reeked of urine and menstrual flow. Haegŭm brought her own blanket and covered Suok *ŏnni*. Yŏnsun did likewise. She herself took the hand that stuck out from the blanket; it felt like bones encased in ice.

"They said I was seven months along." Suok *ŏnni* heaved a sigh; her breath had the strong smell of steamed eggplant. "It was a boy, and one side was black and rotten from head to toe."[12]

Kŭmbok *ŏnni* dabbed at her face and neck with a damp towel.

"If he was seven months, he must have had his fingers?" Suok *ŏnni* said to Kŭmbok *ŏnni*.

"My baby brother came out two months early but his face was fine," mumbled Haegŭm. "Mom asked me to count his fingers, and yup, he had all ten. Then she said to count his toes. I guess she was afraid he was missing something. I told her they were all there. And that's when she told me to give him to her to hold. I think she was really worried. But like I said, his face was fine, and his hair was pretty nice too."

At that point Hanok ŏnni nudged her.

After Suok ŏnni lost the baby her eyes were never the same. Her irises never stayed put but kept rolling upward as though they would disappear forever.

Whenever she had an injection of the dark red, endlessly burning 606, she felt her arm was coming off, it hurt so much.[13] For the next several days, it was like heaven and earth had switched places; she couldn't keep food down and she gave off a pungent, nauseating smell. Her monthly cycle went out of whack. No one told the girls they were being injected with an arsenic compound that could leave them sterile. Not even the nurse who injected them. *Haha* told the girls it was a blood purifier—a flat-out lie.[14]

She detested washing *sakku* as much as getting the 606 shot. What with *haha* badgering the girls to use them sparingly and never handing out enough of them in the first place, the girls would wash and reuse them. The soldiers who had come and gone from them tossed the used *sakku* in the can on their way out. The fishy stink from the *sakku* heaped in the can left the girls retching.[15] After breakfast the girls took their cans to the washing area and cleaned the *sakku* of ejaculate inside and out. After drying them on a sheet of plywood they added a sprinkling of white disinfecting powder. Every time the girls cleaned the *sakku* they would shudder at the thought of all the soldiers who had come and gone from them the previous night. And at the prospect of having to take the same number of soldiers during the night to come.[16] While the *sakku* were drying, the girls were in the yard taking in the sun. But they never had enough time because the soldiers began flocking in at nine in the morning. The enlisted men came between nine and five, the NCOs from five to ten, and the officers from ten to midnight.[17] Some of the officers came in the middle of the night.[18]

That morning, too, the girls washed and hung their *sakku* to dry before gathering in the yard. Punsŏn stretched her legs out toward the sun; for most of the winter she'd been making the rounds of the other girls' rooms to keep herself warm, ever since her body had shut down because of the cold and dampness and she could no longer take men—after which *haha* cut off her supply of hot water for her canister pack and the pea coal for her brazier. Punsŏn used to visit her just long enough to warm her feet with the hot-water pack.[19]

The Manchurian winter was so cold your breath and your pee would turn to ice as soon as you released it. Waking up in the morning, the girls were greeted with a sheet of ice on the window-side wall stretching to the ceiling. They braved the frigid winter with a blanket or two, the hot-water canister, and pea coal. The coal ration from *haha* was barely enough to keep them from freezing to death.

"Mom was about to marry me off," said Kisuk *ŏnni* to the girls huddled in the yard. Another strategy she used to avoid the military police with their red armbands was to hide in the rice chest. Kisuk *ŏnni* also tried hiding in a crematory but was caught and then brought to the comfort station.[20]

From the other girls at the station she learned that fretful parents were quick to try to marry off their daughters—whether to a widower with kids, a shriveled old man, or a man who was missing a leg—anything to prevent them from being taken away. But this was a mistaken assumption, as some girls were taken away in the presence of their husbands.[21] The Japanese soldiers and military police had a sixth sense for ferreting out unmarried girls who tried to disguise themselves as married by wearing their hair in a bun covered by a towel.

"My father faked a marriage report for me," said Hanok ŏnni, eyes half shut from a sleepless night. "Ch'oe was the man's name, he was sixteen years older . . . and I never did meet him face to face. My father made him swear he'd cancel the marriage report if I hooked up with someone I actually liked. So I went around with my hair in a bun, but the village head's wife found out it was a fake marriage and she played a trick on me, said if I worked three years at a needle factory I'd make a pile of money. You see, the village head was Japanese."

"And where are you going to find an unmarried guy, anyway? They'd all been taken away to be soldiers, miners, or factory workers. This friend of mine had a face that was full of life and a wrinkled old man for a husband . . . damn shame!"[22] Tongsuk ŏnni smiled faintly as she said this.

"Damn shame or not, I kind of wish I'd married an old man."[23] Aesun's tone was strained and monotonous; if there is such a thing as a threadbare voice it was hers.

While the girls were being taken away to serve in the Women's Labor Corps or at the comfort stations, the boys were drafted to work in the mines, the steel yards, the ammunition factories, the airports, and the railroad construction sites. Tongsuk ŏnni said her brother left their home village in Nonsan to work in Japan.

"He saw this ad in the paper that an ironworks in Japan was hiring. They needed a hundred men and were providing housing, the same pay the Japanese got, and a certificate once you complete the two-year training period. And he was just itching to learn a trade."

Grudgingly the girls rose and dispersed. What a shame to have to dispense with the warming spring sunshine they'd awaited the whole winter long. They let the sun hit their faces one last time before returning to their rooms.

In no time a flock of soldiers arrived, turning the yard into a sea of yellow. Already they were undoing their gaiters while waiting their turn.

Fifteen men a day was normal, but on Sundays fifty men or more might come and go from a girl.[24]

To save time, instead of taking off their pants, the enlisted men merely unzipped and undid their loincloth.[25] She often felt the dagger sheath on their belts poking her belly.[26]

If the soldiers had trouble penetrating, they applied ointment to the *sakku*.[27]

When a soldier came and went from her, she felt as if a thin strip of flesh had been carved from her privates. After ten men had come and gone from her, she felt there was no flesh left to be carved.

At any given time her vagina would prolapse and not even a needle could penetrate it.[28]

Lacking a calendar, the girls never knew the day of the week or the date and could only assume Sunday had arrived by the number of soldiers who came and went.[29] The days were anonymous, and as they streamed by, the girls broke down.

"Is there ever going to be an end to these fucking guys?"[30] Ch'unhŭi ŏnni would grumble whenever the soldiers surged into the yard.

Wanting to leave the soldiers disgusted with her, she didn't wash her face and didn't comb her hair.

Even so, in no time the soldiers were swarming her and the other girls like fire ants.[31]

If only there was a battle every day. When there was a battle the soldiers didn't come. And if only the soldiers never returned from battle. The soldiers who did return seemed to be in a frenzy, they were so giddy and violent. They were covered with dust from head to toe, they hadn't washed, and they stank. Their arrival transformed the comfort station into a madhouse—in one room a fight between a soldier and a girl, in another room a girl beaten by a soldier she was trying to get away from, a drunk soldier running amok in the next room, a girl sobbing in grief in the next room, a girl haranguing a soldier who didn't want to use a *sakku* . . .

Often soldiers flat-out refused to use a *sakku*. No matter how a girl might plead, saying she'd come down with a terrible disease and didn't want him to catch it, the soldier wasn't about to listen. So what, the soldiers retorted, they might die in battle today, or tomorrow, so why worry about a stupid disease—and then they would pounce. *What if I come down with gonorrhea or syphilis?* Such worries drove her up a wall.

There were soldiers who cried knowing they were going off to battle. One of them, a slightly built youth in a man-sized uniform, clutched her arm as he might have that of a big sister, and sniffled. The mere sight of the Japanese military uniform made her want to throw up, but she soothed him nonetheless: *Come on now, don't cry and just make sure you come back alive.* . . . Even though she wished that none of the Japanese soldiers would come back alive, this soldier, crying like a child, captured her sympathies. She never saw him again and never did learn if he had survived.

During the lull between battles the soldiers were comparatively docile.

The girls also hoped Japan would win the war. Because if it lost they were sure to die, all of them.[32]

Haha's mantra was, "If Japan wins the war, *then* you girls can go home." And they'd be set for life, she added. "Japan wins and I'll send you girls home with enough money to sock away a good-sized patch of paddy land."

It didn't have to be paddy, she would tell herself; a good amount of cotton fabric to take home would do—or enough soybeans to fill the soy-sauce crocks.[33] Yes, better that way than dying there in Manchuria.[34] But the next moment she would wonder what use it would be to go home; considering what she'd done in the comfort station, she'd be better off dead.[35] What would she say to her family? That she'd been working at a thread factory? A silk factory? Maybe she should just tell them she was working at a nice factory? Such thoughts filled her with gloom.

Haha sometimes handpicked half a dozen girls to send to a backcountry outpost. Military transport would be sent for them.

In a makeshift comfort station put together with canvas and plywood partitions, the girls were put to work taking the soldiers. In their bent-leg frog-flipped-over-on-its-back position, the girls took the soldiers all day long. By evening, when the officers summoned the girls to their tents—you wouldn't find them going to the comfort station— they were unable to straighten their legs. Their meals were brought from the canteen and consisted of a couple of spoonfuls of flattened barley with pickled radish on the side. Very rarely they were given thin spinach soup and canned fish.[36] After a week of taking soldiers they returned to the comfort station.[37]

On one such trip to an outpost the truck passed through a Chinese village littered with corpses. The girls saw women and children making their way among the bodies and heard them wailing. The truck drove straight through, crushing arms, legs, and heads. When the wheels ran over a pudgy man's belly and his innards burst out, it was like a full-body shock to the girls.

While she was gazing at a man slumped against the earthen wall of a home, wondering if he was dead or alive, Punsŏn tapped her on the shoulder. "Look, that dog's dragging off a dead boy! Why would it do that?" Punsŏn cocked her head skeptically.

"For food . . . it's probably hungry," Ch'unhui ŏnni said with a pout.

Pongae awoke from a nap with an embarrassed grin. Above a collapsed house fluttered a *Hinomaru* flag the size of a blanket. A barefoot woman standing with a devastated expression before the charred remnants of a home looked with hollow eyes at the girls in the truck.

The truck left the village and in time a river appeared. It was twice as wide as the river in her home village. The near bank was heaped with the branches and trunks of chopped-down trees. Armed soldiers guarded the dock.

A mass of corpses floated down the river, reddening the water, before coming apart at the bow of the ferry taking the girls upstream.[38]

☀

The potato on the round plate is the size of a baby's fist. She looks at the potato, a thread of steam rising from it, as if it's the last meal she'll ever have.

When finally she takes it in her hand, her eyes lose focus and flicker. She holds out the hand with the potato.

"Take it!"

She realizes no one is there but can't take the potato back.

She could have sworn Yŏnsun was across from her.

Yŏnsun, scrawny and malnourished though she was, socked away the hardtack, taffy, and canned goods she got from the soldiers, instead of consuming them herself. She couldn't get over thoughts of her younger siblings, whom she imagined nibbling on cuckoo lilies or wild rose petals when they had nothing to eat. The cuckoo lilies blossomed in early summer around the time the cuckoos could be heard calling, and her siblings ate the tender shoots fresh off the stalk, though they left a bitter taste. Yŏnsun said she would ask the lieutenant who was one of her regulars to have her stash sent home. He had a daughter the same age as Yŏnsun. One day he went off to battle and didn't return.[39] Not long after, Yŏnsun was sent elsewhere. Cheekbones jutting from hollowed cheeks, Yŏnsun hugged her bundle tightly as she climbed into the truck.

The other girls had gathered in the yard to see her off. "She was so pretty when she got here and now look at her, the poor thing!"

"Did they really cut her open to get rid of her baby?"[40]

When the soldiers they'd gotten used to seeing didn't show up over a period of time, the girls assumed they'd been killed in battle.

She pinches off a tiny chunk of the potato and brings it to her mouth.

The girls knew what it meant to be hungry.

They knew from the time they were in their mother's womb.

They knew even before their mouths were formed.

There was hunger at the Manchurian comfort station too. *Haha* served tin bowls of gruel to the girls for breakfast. The gruel was clear as water, so clear the girls could see their entire face reflected in it,[41] and the only side dish was pasty-looking *kimchi* that was going bad. More often than not it was weevils or maggots floating to the surface of the gruel instead of bits of meat. When the gruel was gone the girls scooped at their face reflected in the bottom of the bowl. But all the scooping in the world could never fill them.

The rice balls were generally spoiled in summer and frozen in winter. But regardless of condition they weren't served to the girls who couldn't take soldiers because they'd caught a venereal disease. Those girls instead would eat the hardtack given them by the soldiers, soaking it first in water to make it last longer. Soaking made the hardtack swell up until it resembled a hunk of steamed pork.

Dinner was almost always wheat gruel made by boiling salted clumps of dough. Eating a bowl of it left the girls with the smell of wallpaper paste coming from their mouth.[42] With dinner constantly interrupted by the arrival of soldiers, even this meager fare was eaten only a few spoonfuls at a time. She often cooks noodles for herself but never soup with wheat dumplings, which reminds her of the wheat gruel.

On the twice-monthly volunteer days the girls were graced with *miso* soup, however watery it might be, and only had to take soldiers in the evening. On these days *otosan* mustered the girls and loaded them into the cargo truck. A half-hour ride brought them to a lone, dreary canvas structure that resembled a neglected workshop storage shed. Inside, the girls sat across from each other on planks and repaired soldiers' uniforms—mending caps and pants and darning socks. She wished she were mending her father's *chŏgori* instead. Or her brother's *chŏgori*. Or her mother's quilted socks. . . . She never understood why the girls had to mend the uniforms on top of everything else they did for the soldiers. Why didn't the soldiers' mothers or sisters do the mending? But as vexed as she felt with this chore, she didn't want to take shortcuts what with the deep freeze winter brought to Manchuria. It was so cold that even the cabbage for making *kimchi* turned into icy blocks.

Later she heard that the girls who were taken to Singapore ate rice steamed in bloody water. At the height of the Pacific War with explosions all around, the girls were transported by scooter-trailer to take the soldiers. Late one night six girls huddled in a blacked-out tent were feeding a few handfuls of rice into a canteen when a bomb exploded outside. The freaked-out girls escaped with the canteen, instinctively groping in the dark for water to add to the rice, and were still on the move when day broke. Finally they could cook, but when they saw that the mixture in the canteen was red as the blood of a slaughtered pig they realized that what they had scooped in the dark was blood instead of water. How could they eat *that?* But after talking it over they decided to go ahead rather than risk starving to death, and so they closed their eyes and ate. Six girls avoided starving by eating rice cooked with the blood of a dead person, but only one of those six ended up surviving the war.[43]

※

Sitting in front of the TV and staring at the paper mask, she cocks her head. *Is that supposed to look like my face?* She wonders if her face came to mind when the girl was making the eyes and nose.

She wants to cry but can't. She lowers her head and opens her mouth as wide as a hungry goblin, but not a tear falls. Nor did the passing of her sisters and her older brother bring tears. She was met instead with backbiting from her relatives: her obstinacy had turned her into a spinster for life and left her heartless. For her, though, it was her relentless life that had left her dry-eyed; no amount of pulling on her eyelids would bring tears. She must have cried herself dry back then when she was young, she would tell herself, rather than rationing them throughout her life.[44]

How savage she was; even animals can cry, she reproached herself when her brother's death failed to bring her to tears.

What's the use of living if you can't even measure up to an animal?

What if I saw Kunja—would that bring me to tears? Or Kŭmbok ŏnni? Or T'anshil? Or Sundŏk? . . .

Sundŏk from Hapch'ŏn in South Kyŏngsang Province said she thought she was heading to Inch'ŏn to work as a live-in maid but ended up at the comfort station.

"I left home at age 12 and worked as a maid for a Japanese officer's family. I had no choice because at home we never knew where our next meal was coming from. I cleaned house for them, I did the laundry, I ran errands, I even went to the market. . . . The officer's name was Takeshi. I was there three years and then Takeshi says to me how would I like to go to Inch'ŏn, I could get eight *wŏn* a month as a maid there, you know? Sure, I said, and the next thing I know he sticks twenty-four *wŏn* in my hand, a three-month advance, see? I gave twenty to my mom and kept the rest, bought myself a dress and a pair of white rubber shoes with it—I was *soooo* happy. . . . Mommy came out to the station with me and bought me some crabapples for the trip. If I'd known I was ending up here, I'd have given Mom the other four *wŏn* too. Yeah, I definitely should have given her the whole amount."[45]

From *haha*'s radio came the chirping of a cuckoo.

"Why does that damn cuckoo keep calling?"[46] So saying, Sundŏk pulled her close and began whimpering. She herself felt the same way. Listening to the cuckoo on the radio left her missing Mom and home dearly. *Cuckoo, cuckoo*—the chirping had her weeping in no time.

Tears dribbled down tall Tongsuk ŏnni's broad face too.

"What if I die and never get to see my little brother again?"[47] lamented Hanok ŏnni, sitting out in the hallway with her legs stretched out. He was her only sibling and she'd promised him that when she came back from the needle factory she would buy him a couple of calves.

It was more than ten years ago that Sundŏk visited her in a dream—though in the dream she couldn't immediately recall her name. She was in the kitchen rinsing rice and in popped Sundŏk. She herself had grown old, but Sundŏk was as youthful as she remembered her. And she was wearing the same drab sack dress. Sundŏk disappeared momentarily and she found her sitting demurely next to the window in her bedroom.

"What was your name?" It still hadn't come to mind.

"Yeah, good question, what is it? . . . Maybe a person who doesn't even measure up to a dog or a cat doesn't rate a name, and anyway I can't even remember it.[48] And sometimes my mom's name and my dad's name escape me too."

"Well I don't remember how old I am."

"Same with me. But I was 13 when they took me away—I remember that as clear as day."

"You haven't aged a bit—how can that be?" But far from envying Sundŏk, she felt pity for her. As Sundŏk was getting up to leave, she detained her, saying she should at least have a bite to eat.

"What do you miss the most?"

"Fresh sweet peppers dipped in *toenjang* paste, that's all."

"Not meat?"

"I can't. Remember? Not after I saw them burning all those bodies."

She left to put together a meal, but when she returned with the meal tray Sundŏk had disappeared.

Awakening from her dream, she sobbed for a good long time, thinking Sundŏk had come to say goodbye forever.

Among the women she saw on television was one who couldn't find her way back to Korea after its liberation from Japan. She was in a comfort station in the Heilongjiang area and barely remembered her own name.

Is she still alive? And if so, how old would she be? She has to be the one who was sitting next to me on the train, asking which factory I was going to—just like Haegŭm used to do.

5

WHO COULD HAVE TAKEN MY SHOES? Her face scrunches up as if she's about to cry. Her eyes scan the yard then return to the trash can. *That's right, I hid them behind the trash last night before I went to bed.* She retrieves the shoes and sets them neatly below the edge of the veranda. But she can't put them on, they just don't look like hers, and all she can do is gape at them.

Hmm, maybe the last one left them here? After the next-to-last one passed away and now she's all alone? She must have come by last night and left her shoes.

She wonders if the last one might be T'anshil. Or maybe it's Aesun, who drank the arsenic solution that left her sounding like a parrot when she talked. Or Changshil ŏnni, a helpful shadow for her sister T'anshil, whose sight was dimmed by syphilis—except when Changshil had to take soldiers, and then she felt compelled to get her little sister as far away from herself as she could. For T'anshil it was like having a prosthetic removed.

During all these years she hasn't encountered any of the girls from the Manchuria comfort station. Needless to say, she doesn't know if they're dead or alive, not to mention where they might be or any other particulars.

In the post-Liberation period the girls scattered every which way. Some followed the Japanese soldiers, some remained in China, some died crossing from China back to Korea. In any event the majority ended up dead before their time.

Even while speculating about who might have returned safely, even while visiting the home village of Kunja, whom she missed so terribly, she remained anxious at the possibility of encountering any of the girls by chance. And she's forever on pins and needles thinking, *What if someone finds out I used to be a comfort woman?* And when she's out and about, if she feels someone is giving her a suspicious look she'll disappear into the nearest alley.

※

So there were other comfort stations—she learned this from the girls who had arrived from stations elsewhere. Until then she'd assumed there couldn't possibly be another place like the Manchuria comfort station.

Three years had passed and the number of girls had grown from twenty-five to thirty-two—and this despite the fact that quite a few girls had left. Not that any of them had walked out on her own. Safer to say they had all come down sick and were told to leave. *Haha* made the girls with serious diseases, such as syphilis, use a separate outhouse until they got better, and then they had to take soldiers again. The girls had two chances at this salvage operation; if they were infected a third time, *otosan* would load them into the truck and take them away—or soldiers might show up for that purpose. None of the girls taken away had ever returned. *Haha* was tight-lipped about the fate of the girls, whether they'd gone home or to another comfort station.[1]

And then there were the girls who departed only in death, such as Kisuk *ŏnni*, who had bled to death after taking opium.

The girls who left or died were invariably replaced. Some of the new arrivals were as oblivious as she had been about their duties at the comfort station; others had circulated among other comfort stations.

Atarashino kita! "A new shipment!" There was an instant buzz among the soldiers.

Depending on where a new girl was from, the others might pelt her with questions: "What's happening in Taegu?" "How's life in Pusan?"[2]

Sisters T'anshil and Changshil were among the transplants. *Otosan* had brought them not long after Sŏksun *ŏnni*'s death. Ch'unhŭi *ŏnni* heard him boasting to *haha* that he'd gotten two for the price of one.

"That one doesn't know a thing—show her," *haha* would order the girls. After which the girls would demonstrate for the new arrival, unrolling a *sakku* over their thumb as *haha* had done for them.

"You have to *tell* them to use it, otherwise someone gets sick."[3] Kŭmbok *ŏnni* would drill this into the new girls.

Among the new arrivals was a 12-year-old. Like most girls she wore a *ch'ima* the color of ink, and it smelled of the wild greens of her native village—shepherd's purse, chives, mugwort . . .

"How could they take you away, you're just a baby?" asked Kŭmbok *ŏnni*, sprawled out on the floor from the effects of her 606 shot.

"They got me at the village well when I was fetching water," drawled the new girl as if talking in her sleep. "I filled my water jar and was about to set it on my head when someone grabbed me by the shoulder. It was a soldier with a star right here, and he was wearing a sword, and he had such mean eyes—"

"Sweetie," interrupted pockmarked Pongae, who was scratching her sallow, lumpy face. "What's your name?"

"Yŏngsun. What is this place anyway?"[4] The girl seemed to come out of her trance, her eyes widening.

"It's a *ppiya*," growled opium-laden Hunam *ŏnni*, whose complexion was the color of lead.

Ppiya was what the girls called the comfort station. The term was used by *haha, otosan*, the Japanese soldiers, and the Chinese as well. The girls were *Chosen ppi*. This was the expression she herself most hated hearing, once she learned that *ppi* was Chinese for "cunt." Among the vulgarities she'd learned, *Chosen ppi* was the foulest and most degrading.

"*Ppiya*? What's that?"

"It's a place where soldiers come and you sleep with them," said Yŏnsun as she puffed on one of the cigarettes she'd been given by a soldier. A rat could be heard squeaking from the kitchen. Maybe the rat trap was working?

"Soldiers? What if they shoot me? Then I won't be able to take care of them."[5]

Tongsuk *ŏnni* chuckled.

"You're a little chick, they won't kill you," said Haegŭm.

Yŏngsun seemed relieved, but the next moment was bawling that she wanted to go home.

"Crying won't get you anywhere," said T'anshil, her dim gaze directed at the ceiling where rats were scampering about.

"You can check in any time you want, but you can never leave,"[6] said Changshil *ŏnni*. Her lips were the color of an eggplant. The previous night a noncommissioned officer had knocked out three of her front teeth. He'd put his finger in her vagina and was trying to wiggle it around when she said, "Why don't you try that on your mother instead?" Earning her a beating from the enraged soldier. By the time she left the comfort station she had lost almost all her teeth.[7] *Haha* gave Yŏngsun the name Gohana, Japanese for "little flower," and sent her to a vacant room. The girls didn't tell Yŏngsun it was the room where Kisuk *ŏnni* had died. Yŏngsun took soldiers on the same tatami mat that Kisuk *ŏnni* had used. She wore Kisuk *ŏnni's* dress, used Kisuk *ŏnni's* leftover tissue, and used the *sakku* that Kisuk *ŏnni* had cleaned and left out to dry.

The next morning Yŏngsun visited each of the other girls, crying all the while.

One day Tongsuk *ŏnni* coughed up blood the deep red color of wild strawberries. Her face turned ashen and the next they knew, she was having trouble walking. The girls whispered among themselves that she'd come down with lung disease.

"It's all those damn soldiers she had to take, that's why," said Haegŭm, her hands trembling more violently than usual as she rinsed her *sakku*.

"Next it'll be us," said Punsŏn as she washed her *sakku* number fifteen.

"We'll be useless down below," said Ch'unhŭi *ŏnni* as she tore a *sakku* apart instead of washing it.

Tongsuk *ŏnni's* cough got worse, but still *haha* made her take soldiers. After she coughed blood while taking a soldier *haha* turned the nameplate on her door backside out. And to make sure the other girls wouldn't catch her ailment, *haha* prevented them from visiting her. From time to time the girls could hear Tongsuk *ŏnni* coughing her lungs out, and all day long her room bore a somber chill along with a bloody stink. The girls would peep into Tongsuk ŏnni's room whenever *haha* wasn't looking.

The frosts arrived and Tongsuk ŏnni's condition deteriorated rapidly.

Kŭmbok ŏnni stopped to see *haha* on her way to the wash area with a tin washbasin containing a bloody towel from Tongsuk ŏnni's room.

"Can't you send her home?"

"I'm not sending her anywhere until she pays off her debt."

Even while Tongsuk ŏnni was coughing the last of her lifeblood, her debt continued to swell like a cocoon being spun by a silkworm.

"Can't I pay it off for her?"

"Do you have any idea how much you owe us? You pay off *your* debt first and then I'll listen to you!" And with that *haha* turned and disappeared. Even an imminent death wouldn't make her more generous.

An officer on horseback arrived in the middle of the night to find her in bed weeping. *Watashiga anatani jihi o hodokosu daro!* he boasted. "I bestow on you my charity!" He followed by giving her a mildewed Japanese banknote. When that didn't bring a stop to her weeping, he snarled, *Jihi o kotowaru nante!* "Is that how you respond to my charity!" The enraged officer sat her up and slapped her back and forth. *Chosenjini chihio hodokusuyori inuni hodokushita houga ii!* "Better to give charity to a dog than a Korean!"

And then he stripped her naked and ordered her to give him a massage.[8] Crouching like a sick kitten on his back, she massaged his shoulders.

After he'd fallen asleep she left to go to the toilet. Along the way and shivering with cold, she looked into Tongsuk ŏnni's room. Kŭmbok ŏnni was at Tongsuk ŏnni's bedside watching over her. Eerie moonlight filtered through the ice-glazed window. The station was tranquil, as if everyone was gone and only the three of them were left. Not even the sound of breathing could be heard from Ch'unhǔi ŏnni's room across the way, where earlier around midnight a bestial wail had escaped, as if she were being taken to a slaughterhouse.

Rubbing the instep of her frozen foot against the back of her other leg, she gazed at Tongsuk ŏnni's brazier. Amid the white ash a single coal glowed faintly. It looked to her like the heart of a dying hare left unnoticed among the spent coals. The least she could do was give Tongsuk ŏnni some coal, but she had none. She had the elusive sensation that the air in the room was changing along with the waning of the glow.

"Is she sleeping?"

"She just now dropped off. . . . Sure is pretty."

She could see Tongsuk ŏnni's breath, blossoming like a white paper flower.

She looked uncomprehendingly at Kǔmbok ŏnni.

"Her face, I mean."

Over Kǔmbok ŏnni's shoulder she could see Tongsuk ŏnni's face. It was devoid of expression. Kǔmbok ŏnni reached out and caressed the expressionless face. The bloody stench from the room was painfully nauseating and forced her to stifle her breathing.

"You should get some sleep, ŏnni," she managed to say.

"You're right." But now she was combing Tongsuk ŏnni's hair with her fingers, like a mother sending off a daughter at daybreak to her new in-laws in a far-off place. Tongsuk ŏnni, who had just now dropped off to sleep, never woke up.

"Ŏnni . . . ŏnni!" No matter how Aesun called, her parrot voice couldn't awaken Tongsuk ŏnni. Outside in the hall T'anshil's head poked out from her room and moved back and forth as she wondered what was happening. But the next moment her confused expression gave way to a bright smile as if she had caught sight of a welcome presence. Her dim eyes would apprehend things the other girls couldn't see. She once said she saw a girl standing naked on the other side of the barbed wire, only to learn later that this must have been Sŏksun ŏnni, who had died before T'anshil arrived.

Yŏngsun, unable to relieve herself for four days because of her prolapsed privates, went down the hall crying. Changshil ŏnni had contracted syphilis and her nameplate had been turned inside out. Ch'unhŭi ŏnni emerged from her room scratching her head. Because she never washed her face, she had the look of someone who had caught the plague. Sitting across from each other, legs spread, Yŏnsun and Haegŭm picked crab lice from each other's pubic hair with tweezers.

"We're going to survive, we're going to make it back home," said Yŏnsun.

"And we're never going to forget each other," said Haegŭm.

The crab lice lived in the pubic hair and came with the soldiers. Their bites left the privates an angry red, itchy and swollen. In their spare time the girls spread their legs and picked lice from each other.[9]

Yŏnsun and Haegŭm pledged themselves to sisterhood and sealed the pledge by giving each other a blue, threadlike tattoo.[10]

Aesun emerged bawling, "Tongsuk ŏnni's dead!"

Kŭmbok ŏnni dressed Tongsuk ŏnni in the best preserved of her garments. Tongsuk ŏnni's long eyelashes seemed to twitch faintly, like the second hand of a clock. *Maybe she's still alive?* she herself wondered.

No flowers were available and so the girls opened their mouths and adorned Tongsuk ŏnni with a bouquet of vapor blossoms. Suok ŏnni opened her mouth and from between her buck teeth came tiny white flowers resembling those of chili pepper plants. Yŏnsun and Haegŭm mingled their breath to produce a peony. Perched above Tongsuk *ŏnni's* face, Kŭmbok *ŏnni* was painstakingly fashioning a huge flower that resembled a snowball viburnum.

Otosan burned Tongsuk *ŏnni's* corpse. When a girl died he would roll up the body in a straw mat and either toss it into the empty fields or burn it.

While the girls were taking soldiers, they could hear the crackling of the fire and smell Tongsuk *ŏnni's* burning body. The bursting of her swollen stomach and the cracking of her burning bones circulated in the heavens before settling in the girls' ears.[11]

Her burning body smelled like rotting fish.[12]

And it was just their luck that the soldiers surged in nonstop that day. The girls had to skip dinner to take them. The soldiers had just returned from battle and smelled like cow dung. Their red, crater-like eyes still bore a bloodthirsty tinge, and they were rabid as hunting dogs. A soldier missing a boot entered her, and the next moment opened his maw and vomited all over her face. A lieutenant with wavy hair entered her making a sound with his mouth like the buzzing of a blowfly. A soldier bit her ear upon mounting her, and she imagined him turning into a mad dog. Another soldier's contorted face she saw as a reflection from the surface of the flickering light bulb.

Not until dawn was she able to visit the site where Tongsuk *ŏnni* had been burned. Kŭmbok *ŏnni* and Punsŏn were already there. Kŭmbok *ŏnni* stepped into the ash, each step producing a silvery fluff. In the light of dawn Kŭmbok *ŏnni's* thighs beneath her sack dress were so pale you could see her veins. Kŭmbok *ŏnni* bent over to pick up something—a round, grayish fragment of Tongsuk *ŏnni's* skull that gave off a ghostly white glint in the dawn light. Kŭmbok *ŏnni* brushed the ash from the fragment before wrapping it in a cotton cloth and bringing it to her chest. "It's still warm," she murmured, "like her heart."

Kŭmbok ŏnni kept the fragment in the wooden box that contained her clothing. A year later when she left the comfort station it was the first item she packed in her cloth bundle. She said if she made it back home she would go to Tongsuk ŏnni's home village and bury it there.[13]

She turned in to haha the mildewed Japanese banknote given her by the officer, along with the tickets she'd collected the previous day. Japanese bills were worthless scraps of paper to the girls, who had no use for them.

From Pongae's room came the cajoling voice of Kŭmbok ŏnni: "What's the matter with you? We don't have to die here, you know."

"What kind of a future do I have?" Pongae was on drugs.

"We have to do whatever it takes to get back home—don't you want that?"

"But ŏnni, how can I look my mom in the face?"

"Wake up, girl. You don't want to die like a dog out here in the middle of nowhere."

Pongae went off opium and took up tobacco and strong liquor instead.

The girls had heard of comfort stations elsewhere, and on one of their trips to the Chinese village they saw one. Whenever the girls had to go to an outpost, haha would take them to the bathhouse in the village. There they scrubbed each other clean, dead skin and all, while haha for her part had a Chinese girl do it.

On this particular trip Pokcha ŏnni indicated a three-story brick building on a busy street and told the girls about it. Pokcha ŏnni had arrived after Tongsuk ŏnni died. The so-called atarashi, "new shipment," she looked as old as haha. Pokcha ŏnni didn't ask what she was supposed to do there and didn't go around to the other girls' rooms in tears the next morning.

"There are girls from back home there."

The brick building had wide, squat windows at regular intervals on each floor, but the windows had odd-looking grates over them.[14] The metal gate to the building was like a folding door, and there was a sign made of wood on one of the posts. She herself couldn't read Chinese and had no idea what the column of characters on the sign meant. Then the gate opened and an older girl rushed out. The girl was wearing a *kimono*, but she could tell the girl was from Korea. She could spot the ones from back home, whether they wore *kimono* or *qipao*. Across the street the girl went, toward a place that looked like a shop. Back she ran and as soon as she was through the gate it clanked shut as if it would never open again.

"It used to be an inn, and then the Japanese took it over."

Pokcha *ŏnni* went on to say the Chinese owner had hung himself from the stairs.

"The Japanese soldiers cut open a pregnant Chinese woman and took out her baby," said Pongae.

"I saw six Japanese soldiers rape a Chinese woman behind the train station in Harbin," said Pokcha *ŏnni*. "They saw her walking by and went after her like a pack of mad dogs. She was terrified and tried her best to get away, but she must have had bound feet because she took only a few steps before they caught up with her. Some Chinese men were nearby, but do you think they cared? All they did was gawk."

At the thatch-roofed building where the girls had a weekly medical exam for venereal disease, they sometimes saw girls who worked at other stations.

Once they arrived to see a line of new faces in front of the building. A man in a military uniform was haranguing one of them, a girl whose face was the color of an orange and who couldn't stand up straight.

"These Korean bitches are hopeless,"[15] the man said, then hit the tottering girl in the head with his baton. The girl spun once like a slow-motion top, fell to her knees, then collapsed to the ground. "Leave her alone—she can die for all I care,"[16] he barked when the other girls went to her aid.

She noticed in the line three girls linked at the wrist by a rope, looking like a string of dried fish.[17] Presumably the rope was to prevent them from escaping.

She overheard *otosan* talking with the man. She had a basic understanding of Japanese by then, thanks to *haha*'s insistence that the girls speak Japanese. *Haha* also had Kisuk ŏnni and Sundŏk, who knew Japanese, teach the girls who didn't. The first phrase she learned was *Irasayemase!* "Welcome!" This was how they were to greet the soldiers arriving at the comfort station.[18]

"How are the girls at your place?" *otosan* asked the man who looked like a soldier. "Are they giving you any trouble?"

"Those three are from Kyesŏng and they stick together—they're always up to no good."

"How much did they cost?"

"I paid two hundred for one of them, a hundred for that one, and one-fifty for the third one."[19]

One day when she'd been at the comfort station about three years, *haha* assembled the girls and asked, "Who wants to go Singaporu?"

"Singaporu?"

"Tell me if you want to go, and I'll send you there."

The girls exchanged whispers while trying to read *haha*'s intentions.

"Where's Singapore?"

"I think it's somewhere down south."

"Then it must be warm there."

Suok *ŏnni* kept mum, but *haha* told her to go to Singapore anyway.[20] The next morning *haha* handed a bundle to each of the girls bound for Singapore.

Kŭmbok *ŏnni* was among those girls. She herself was fond of Kŭmbok *ŏnni*, who was four years older and like a big sister to her. Kŭmbok *ŏnni* was from Angang, near the city of Kyŏngju, and was compassionate and attentive to the other girls. In need of food, her mother sent her and her younger sister out to forage in the hills, where they were kidnapped by soldiers. The two girls got separated and Kŭmbok *ŏnni* didn't know if her sister was dead or alive. Seeing that she herself was the spitting image of her sister, she took her under her wing.

On the day of departure for Singapore she would gladly have given up one of her arms instead of Kŭmbok *ŏnni*. But when Kŭmbok *ŏnni* reiterated to her before leaving, "Just do what *haha* says,"[21] it sounded servile and so she pretended not to hear.

At the comfort station the girls were tormented by gonorrhea or syphilis. But there was something equally painful. Haegŭm, who had come down with a toothache so excruciating it had her thrashing in pain in the hall, was writing something on the ground with her finger, pressing so hard that dirt got wedged beneath her fingernail. She herself could barely identify numbers, but Haegŭm was literate enough to know how to write her name.[22]

She knew Haegŭm was writing a word, but she couldn't read it.

"What are you writing?"

"'Land.'" And then Haegŭm looked up as if the land was somewhere beyond the sky.

Sundown left the girls wanting desperately to return home. For that's when the girls had had chores to do: bringing in the laundry, feeding the livestock, grinding the barley, lighting a fire in the firebox.

She went to the storage room next to the kitchen and there she found Yŏngsun crying over a bowl of wheat gruel. Yŏngsun was always wishing she could go home to fetch the water. She was the only one left in the family who could do this chore, and it was at the village well that she'd been kidnapped. Her mother had fallen ill and died when Yŏngsun was 5, after which she was raised by her grandmother. Here at the comfort station she had just turned 13.

"I don't know what she had, she just wasted away. I remember her going around with a bundle on her head and me on her back—she was selling combs, hairpins, fabrics, and such. . . . And then she passed and my grandmother raised me. If one of the neighbor families was having a celebration, Grandmother would be helping them all day and then bring home some rice cake and fried cakes—wanting to feed me, you know."

Listening to Yŏngsun's story, Yŏnsun broke into tears at the thought of her younger siblings having to do the house-to-house begging now that she was gone.

Whenever the sky was blue and cloudless she herself practically went insane at the thought of the green barley fields back home.

Escaping from the comfort station was a constant desire, but no girl had ever succeeded. There were girls who tried, but they were caught and brought back.

One of the girls had run off on the way back from the regular gynecological checkup at the thatch-roofed building. She was caught not by *otosan* but by the MPs. *Otosan* hauled her out of the truck and dumped her in the yard. Her sack dress was ripped and torn, and she'd been beaten bloody.

"Chop her feet off so she won't do it again," *haha* ordered him.

He pulled out his dagger and for all intents looked ready to show the girls exactly what to expect should anyone else run off. But the girls couldn't look her way and instead looked off in the distance as if betting who could cast the farthest gaze.

With his dagger *otosan* left the would-be runaway with a gash across the ankle.[23]

❋

She still can't get her feet into her shoes, feeling the shoes belong to someone else. The edge of the veranda where she's standing feels like a drop-off to a bottomless pit, and by reflex her toes tense up. Her socks are old and have lost their elasticity and they've slipped below her ankles. As she pulls the right sock up, she stops to feel her ankle bone.

Above the bone is a line you might think was left by an elastic band, but actually it's a scar left by something sharp, a knife perhaps.

She passes her hand across the scar, then opens her mouth and a shriek bursts out. *That was me who had her ankle sliced open at the comfort station!*

When *otosan*'s knife dug into her ankle she blacked out from the unbearable horror and pain. Later she learned from the girls that they were sure she was going to bleed to death.

Two hundred thousand—was it that many? So that's why they took girls as young as 12 or even 11.

She wonders how it was possible so many could be taken. Not two hundred thousand chickens, but two hundred thousand *people*. When she heard on the television that the number of former comfort women had reached two hundred thousand, she couldn't believe it and so she called to mind each of the girls at the Manchuria station and tried to count them. During her seven years there, some fifty girls had passed through. Some of them had been paid for.

When Hanok *ŏnni* said she wanted to leave, *haha* responded, "Then you'll have to pay off your debt."

"How much is my debt?"

"Two thousand *yen*."[24]

The girls weren't aware they had run up a debt—for the sack dress *haha* made them wear; the gruel infested with weevils that resembled black sesame seeds; the barley balls frozen hard as iron; the coarse, dark toilet tissue; the menstrual pads; the hot-water canister; the pea coal for their brazier; the opium brought by *otosan*; all that and everything else.

She herself wondered about the amount of her debt but dared not ask.

For *haha*, coming up with the girls' debt was easier than pricing a pig or cow for sale at the market. No need for the scales, an abacus, or knowledge of a going price. All she had to do was declare that a girl's debt was such-and-such and that was it.[25]

She herself didn't know that the place she had come to was called a comfort station, only that once you were there you took Japanese soldiers. The same for the three-story brick building in the Chinese village. Not until she was older did she understand what a comfort station and a comfort woman were. Until then she assumed the place she was in was like a brothel.[26] No one told her she was at a comfort station or that she was a victimized comfort woman.

After all, *haha* referred to the soldiers as customers.

Take care of the customers, she would say to the girls when a mass of soldiers arrived.

Not until they arrived at the Manchuria comfort station did the girls imagine there were such places in this world.[27]

The soldiers always showed up with a beige-colored ticket one fourth the size of a flower card.[28]

The soldiers bought these tickets from *haha*. Each girl collected her tickets and took them to *haha*. The girls never kept this form of payment from the soldiers coming and going from their bodies. And even if they had, why bother, to the girls they were nothing but scraps of paper. The tickets were like money to the soldiers. But they weren't real money and so the girls couldn't use them to buy clothing, rice cakes, and such.

Haha could tell by the number of tickets a girl gave her how many soldiers she'd taken the previous day. She also posted a graph ranking the girls by their productivity.[29] The girl who turned in the fewest tickets had to skip a meal and clean the outhouse instead. The most productive girl was presented with the finest clothing *haha* had on hand as well as extra food items such as canned goods.[30] For *haha* tickets meant cash since she would sell them back to the soldiers.

An officer once gave her a Manchurian banknote. She gave it to *haha* along with her tickets for the day. To the girls, paper money was just that, paper, just like the tickets. She and the other girls had no idea of the value of money.[31]

Some soldiers tossed their ticket in the *sakku* can. She hated fishing a ticket from the gross-smelling container; even worse, she had to wipe the slime from it. There were times she'd thrown her tickets away in the outhouse.

When the numbers of tickets *haha* received for the previous day didn't match the numbers of tickets she'd sold, she summoned the girls and made them kneel in the yard. *Otosan* was waiting, club in hand, and gave each girl a whack on the thigh, leaving a bruise resembling a tire track.

She herself tended to bring in fewer tickets than the other girls. *Haha* didn't try to hide her displeasure. Once on her way back from the outhouse she stopped to gaze at an enchantingly bright moon, earning her a punch in the head from *haha*, who followed with, "Don't think too hard."

Several days later she was washing her hair and muttering when *haha* appeared with her laundry stick and hit her across the back. "Who do you think you're cussing at?"

She feared *haha* more than the soldiers.[32]

Once when a tubal infection prevented her from taking soldiers and she'd turned in no tickets for four days running, *haha* erupted: "Keep playing sick and I'll send you away for good!"

This repeated threat scared her more than anything, more than the prospect of punishment for a failed attempt at escape—and she never gave up wanting to escape. For in her mind, what *haha* meant by "send you away for good" was "kill you once and for all."

The girls were never paid by the soldiers they took, but she heard other girls say they had been paid.[33] Those girls said that the tickets were payment for sex, even though you couldn't exchange them for rice grain, clothing, or rubber shoes.

Never at the comfort station had she taken a soldier because she wanted to, or in exchange for money. She would lie on her back like a corpse while the soldiers did what they had come for and left. There were guys who shot as soon they entered her, guys who shot while waiting their turn out in the hall, guys who barged in and pulled the guy on top of her away.[34]

The soldiers had at Ch'unhŭi *ŏnni*, bloody privates and all, as soon as she returned from her abortion.[35]

She knows that some girls who were comfort women received money. A girl who was at a Singapore comfort station, for example, said the girls there were given 60 percent of what the soldiers paid. And so she took in as many men as her body could handle, to rake in as much money as possible—by then she'd spent three years at a Guangdong comfort station, after being promised a factory job, and she was already a fallen woman. What with Japan emphasizing the need to save in order to fill the national war chest, she deposited her comfort station earnings in a military postal savings account under her Japanese name of Kimiko. By the end of the war she had saved up a tidy sum, but then the war ended and her account was frozen. She brought her bankbook back home to Korea just in case, but when she went to Japan and her bank refused to let her make a withdrawal, she ripped up the bankbook.[36]

✳

There were two hundred thousand of them, she had heard. But only twenty thousand returned after Liberation from Japan.

More dismaying than the fact that she is one of two hundred thousand comfort women is the realization that she is one of only twenty thousand who made it back home. *That's one tenth, or one out of ten. . . . Did I get that right? Only one out of ten survived? How could that be?*

She wonders if Hunam *ŏnni* made it back.

Hunam *ŏnni* was five years older and shot herself up with opium five times a day. When it got to the point that she spent all day crying in bed, regardless of the soldiers coming and going from her body, *otosan* took her by the hair and dragged her outside as if she were a straw mat and dumped her out on the barren plains, while the other girls looked on from inside the barbed wire. And on that particular day it was overcast and blustery. The winds that blew in Manchuria smelled of horses. A sea of birds black as coal flocked toward Hunam *ŏnni* as if mistaking her bawling for a birdcall.[37]

Ch'unhŭi *ŏnni* plopped down. "See? We'll never walk out of here alive."[38]

The next morning when the girls emerged from their rooms for breakfast, Hunam *ŏnni* had disappeared from the plains. *Haha's* daughters yapped about a girl being taken away by the Red Beards, the horse-riding bandits.

Sundŏk was addicted as well and her face was a bilious dark color. She would cling to *otosan* begging him to save her. "Sure, I can save you," he would coo before injecting her.[39]

She herself couldn't endure, no way could she endure, and so she had herself injected too.[40] Which got rid of the pain down below, no matter how she bled, and left her oblivious to the number of soldiers who came and went from her. The high left her feeling life was worth living, but when the drug wore off, she felt a crushing pain all over and couldn't focus. At first one shot a day would tide her over, but then she'd have to add a second, and on Saturdays and Sundays when the soldiers swarmed in like fire ants, she would need five. She finally snapped out of it when she saw Hunam *ŏnni* dumped in the wilds, and she quit. From then on, if she found herself craving opium, she smoked or drank instead.[41]

☀

Around the time the flock of soldiers was expected, Pokcha *ŏnni* would yell into the hallway, "Girls, an invasion from the south!"[42]

She herself found this more frightening than she would have a warning that someone was coming to kill her.

Otosan took Miok *ŏnni* for the regular checkup and was informed she was pregnant but the baby was too far along to abort; he made her continue to take soldiers anyway. Miok *ŏnni* assumed the baby was dead already, but her tummy grew larger by the day.

"Do you think she'll really have a baby?" she herself was asked by Kunja, who was rinsing *sakku* in the wash area. Kunja had arrived with Miok *ŏnni*. She herself was the same age as Kunja and had instantly grown close to her.

She herself had a birthmark-like bruise on her face. From a soldier who hit her after seeing her using part of a gaiter as a menstrual pad. He swore it was bad luck.[43]

Haha always left the girls short of supplies. When their toothpaste ran out, the girls used salt instead.

"Even if she does, it probably won't be healthy," Hanok *ŏnni* chimed in.

Miok *ŏnni* had told them she was in a place called Heilongjiang before coming here. She was locked up in a room like a pigsty and that's where she took soldiers. And she was fed like a pig or a cow, her meal of millet pushed through an opening in her door. When she needed to relieve herself she had to holler to the soldier on guard duty to bring a can.[44] Holding it in until the can arrived was as difficult as taking the soldiers.

Pokcha ŏnni arrived with her sakku can, hobbling from a stab wound to her thigh by a drunken soldier.

❀

Haegŭm told everyone at breakfast that her father had visited her in a dream.

"Sweetie, what are you doing in such a frigid place?" her father had said.

"Oh hi, Dad. How's Mom?"

"Your grandma—her mom—is dying, so she went home to check on her."

Her father must have died, he was always having coughing fits, said Haegŭm, and then she broke into tears.[45]

❀

Punsŏn had a telegram sent to her home with the help of a regular customer, the field postmaster. The postmaster said he was from Tokyo and had graduated from Waseda University. After completing his military service he found a job in the postal service and was stationed at the field post office in far-off Manchuria. He sent the telegram for her.[46]

Punsŏn was illiterate and had to dictate the contents of the telegram to Kŭmbok ŏnni:

Working at silk factory. Take care till my return. Don't write back.[47]

Sometime later Punsŏn received two telegrams from home, brought by the postmaster. They had been sent a month apart but arrived together.

Mother dying.[48]

Mother dead.[49]

6

SHE IS SITTING on the veranda, legs drawn up, clasped hands resting on her thighs. Her eyes carve out a spot in the air. "As long as she's still alive, as long as the last one is still alive . . ."[1] She murmurs the words so softly she can't hear them.

A face pops into sight above the wall. She startles, wondering if it's her nephew, then realizes it's the meterman. After craning his neck to read the meter, he puts something dark and square up to his eyes and slowly directs it toward her. *Binoculars!* She flinches.

"Wow—look at all that!" He produces a toothy grin.

She just looks at him.

"Your face is right under my nose. You must've been quite the beauty back in prime time. Guys in the village lined up to get a look at you, right?"

She waves off his hitting on her, it's unsettling. *They sure did! They lined up in front of every room. One goes out, another one comes in.*[2]

"Glad I kept this, I still get good use out of it. All these weasels, when they hear me knocking, they play deaf and dumb. How am I supposed to read the meter if I can't get in? So you can imagine why I keep it handy."

She doesn't respond.

"Every damn gate around here is locked . . . makes me wonder what they're up to inside."

It sounds as if he's complaining about her, and she tingles with guilt. A few months ago she was lying in her room and heard someone calling out persistently. Only half awake, she thought it was the television. Even after realizing it was the meterman she remained still, gazing at the ceiling, as if transfixed by a nightmare. She stayed inside even after he grew tired of rattling the gate and left.

"I can tell which homes are occupied and which aren't, but some of the occupied ones look dead. Guy like me, I get the willies going into those places."

She can understand. Here in 15-*bŏnji* some of the occupied homes really do look empty. Those are the homes that leave her tensed up when she's passing by, much more so than the vacant houses.

"You're using twice as much electricity as last month."

"Oh?"

Her nephew has set up automatic payments for the utility bills. Double the usage probably means double the electric bill. Her nephew will be wondering. The thing is, she didn't use more electricity than the previous month, maybe just a tad more television viewing to catch any news about the last one. In the past she used to leave the television on morning and evening. Her appliances are just like those of other households—television, rice cooker, freezer, and small washer. And even in the dog days of August she doesn't touch the electric fan.

"That's odd. Are you sure?"

"*Halmŏni*, the meter doesn't lie."

"Say, young man, twenty thousand out of two hundred thousand, is that one tenth?"

"Twenty thousand out of two hundred thousand?"

"Yes . . . twenty thousand out of two hundred thousand . . ."

"What's that all about?"

Flustered by the question, she clamps her mouth shut.

"You mean someone's hiring twenty thousand and two hundred thousand applied? Hell, two hundred thousand is the population of a small or medium-sized city . . ."

Regretting her question, she keeps mum.

"How come you're clenching your fists?"

"So I won't lose the snails . . ." The words pop out before she realizes it. *Oh no.* She can't finish the sentence.

"Snails?" Suddenly the playful smile is gone. He inspects her.

"Uh, nothing . . ."

"You said something about snails . . ."

"Did I?"

"*Halmŏni*, why don't you talk with your children about a dementia checkup? My mother-in-law just had one. What I've learned is that with dementia, like every other condition, early detection is best."

She's still not responding. With a smug expression he leaves.

She waits until his footsteps have trailed off down the alley, then opens her left fist. *Where did they go?* She gazes searchingly at her palm.

She and some other girls were at an outpost high in the hills. At nightfall the soldiers called the girls to warm themselves around the campfire. The girls gathered in a circle around the toasty fire. Their pale faces turned rosy. A soldier passed around a canteen of *gaoliang*. After two rounds of the strong spirit Hyangsuk launched into a song she liked to sing. She'd learned it from a kamikaze pilot when she was at a Taiwan comfort station.

"Take off bravely, over the bamboo groove, over the golden waves and silver clouds. No one is there to send me off or wish me luck, no one except my Yuriko, you're the only one . . ."[3] Yuriko was Hyangsuk's Japanese name.

The chattering girls started to cackle and the soldiers chuckled.

She herself was the least worked up. Mopey-faced, she cast her gaze among the girls and soldiers and beheld the smiling face of a dead girl. It was Kisuk ŏnni, who had bled to death in an opium-induced stupor.

She was trying to return the smile when a soldier tapped her on the shoulder. She turned to see the man offering her the canteen.

As she grabbed it she grumbled, "Drop dead, you fucking idiot!"[4]

The soldier's face crumbled and a slap landed on her face. The canteen was knocked to the ground. The only Korean the Japanese soldiers could understand were curse words.

※

A name catches in a recess of her memory and her lips twitch and then release a moan that verges on a lament. That girl disappeared one day without saying goodbye. She heard hushed talk among the girls washing their *sakku* that the girl was six months pregnant.[5]

He was an officer of short stature with a mustache sparse as toothbrush bristles. Seeing her swollen genitalia were causing her pain, he stuck his penis in her mouth. Startled, she clenched her teeth, leaving deep bite marks on his organ. Cursing in a growl that sounded full of coal dust, he shoved her against the wall and then flung open the door and called *otosan*. *Otosan* rushed in and hauled her out to the yard, where he beat her to a pulp and she lost consciousness.

When she came to, her left arm was woefully swollen, the upper-arm bone fractured and dislocated.

"Oh my, back from the dead." Hanok *ŏnni* was relieved. "It's been two days!"

"We were sure he was going to kill you. It's wonderful to have you back!"[6] said Miok *ŏnni* as she ran her hand down her chest.

Haha made her take soldiers before the fracture healed.[7]

⁂

The days were sweltering and more girls were vexed with sores and pus from their swollen privates. Those who had difficulty walking got around by crawling. If the trip to the outhouse was a chore, they used a can. Yŏngsun's navel turned blackish red from late-stage syphilis.

Miok *ŏnni*'s belly ballooned to the point that she couldn't take soldiers, and every visit to the toilet left her whimpering. She was sure she was pregnant and feared the baby would pop out and fall into the toilet pit, which seemed bottomless. *Haha* switched her to kitchen work. While the other girls were serving the soldiers Miok *ŏnni* gave birth onto a flour sack on the kitchen floor.[8] Less than ten days after the delivery she resumed taking soldiers. While she was on duty the sick girls tended to her baby. When the baby was able to hold his head up, *haha* swaddled him and went off to the Chinese village. Soon the girls were whispering that *haha* had sold the baby to a Chinese quack dentist.

Ch'unhŭi *ŏnni* came unstrung and was seen roaming the hallway in the uniform of a petty officer sleeping in her room.[9] *Haha* made her keep taking soldiers.

"Clean her up, girls!"

Ch'unhŭi *ŏnni* had not washed up, and her crusted face looked like a peanut shell. She herself took Ch'unhŭi *ŏnni* by the wrist and led her to the wash area. She sat her down in front of the faucet and turned the water on.

"Where's my mom? She wasn't there when I woke up . . ." Sooty water dripped into Ch'unhŭi ŏnni's half-open mouth.

"She's out in the fields."

"The fields? What for?"

"To dig some potatoes."

Ch'unhŭi ŏnni's face froze. "Mom, where did you go?" Ch'unhŭi ŏnni said, clinging to her arm.

"I didn't go anywhere," she answered.

"Mom, don't you ever go anywhere without me!"

"Of course I won't."

After breakfast she went back out to the yard and saw *otosan* punching Ch'unhŭi ŏnni in the head.

"Didn't I tell you to stay holed up in your room? Why are you slinking around out here?" Harder and harder he punched her.

Around midnight an officer arrived. He asked her name. She'd taken more than thirty soldiers that day and could barely keep her eyes open.

"Why don't I make a name for you—Takeko." Which increased her stock of names by one.

As much as she'd abandoned hopes of returning home, she couldn't get over envying the girls who could remember their home address.

Kunja gave her home address: "North Kyŏngsang Province, Ch'ilgok County, Chich'ŏn Township . . . you keep going on a sickle-shaped little road and then you'll see my house . . . you can memorize the address for me in case I forget."

She herself learned the address by heart and had a vivid image of Kunja's house in her mind even though she'd never been there. Her home too was at the end of a little road.

Before she knew it, she who had arrived at age 13 at the comfort station in Manchuria was turning 20. In the meantime she had grown about as much as the distance between two knuckles. Of the girls who had come to the comfort station seven years ago, only two remained—she and Aesun. Punsŏn had been taken away by *otosan*. Yŏnsun and Haegŭm with the wrist tattoos declaring their sistership had gone separate ways.

She had been the youngest in the train heading endlessly north seven years ago, and now she was one of the oldest.

Otosan brought two more girls. One of them was 13 and this girl's naïve expression, dark cotton *chŏgori*, and funny-looking ankle-length pants made her look like a ghost of she herself way back then at the Taegu train station.

"How'd you end up here?" Yŏngsun asked the girl. "You're only a baby." A cigarette was burning at the tips of 16-year-old Yŏngsun's fingers. "Well, now that you're here, what can you do? Maybe it's your fate . . ." Yŏngsun puffed on the cigarette and the acrid smoke rose, veiling her face before thinning out.

Haha came up with Japanese names for the new girls. "From now on you're Sadako," she said to one of them, having forgotten that was also Hanok ŏnni's Japanese name.

Hanok ŏnni, sprawled out after returning from her injection at the medical station, was about to burp but instead went into a convulsive shudder when she heard *haha's* shrill voice.

※

It was the summer of 1945 and *haha* was pacing around and sobbing, as was her daughter. A rumor that Japan was losing the war circulated among the girls and made them anxious. They believed the defeat of Japan meant their death.[10]

As she was heading for the toilet, *otosan* gnashed his teeth and barked at her, "You bitch, wait till I kill you!"[11]

The soldiers grew more agitated and violent, giving off a goat-like stink. They often drank alone and then brawled with one another.

Breakfast had long since finished and yet no soldiers had rushed in. The girls were relieved but at the same time nervous—there had been no news of a battle, which would have explained the soldiers' absence. *Haha*'s radio turned mute, and *otosan* drove off in his truck as soon as he finished his breakfast. The girls assumed he'd gone to fetch more girls. The roster of girls had peaked at thirty-nine but that summer had thinned down to thirty-two.

The sun hung high in the sky but still no soldiers showed up. She and Hyangsuk sat across from each other, legs splayed, picking crab lice from each other's pubic hair.

Hyangsuk's cheeks were puffy where an officer had smacked her the night before, making her look like she was sucking on a huge candy. She'd already taken twenty-plus soldiers when the officer arrived, and she felt as pulpy as a sea cucumber. Feeling mistreated and unwelcome, the officer yanked her out of bed and slapped her.[12]

Hyangsuk then opened up to her about being raped on her way to the comfort station. She was on a military train that had set out from P'yŏngyang. Three full days into the trip the train suddenly screeched to a stop. Apart from a freight car she rode in with thirty other girls, the train was packed with soldiers and military supplies. The freight car had no windows—not that there was anywhere they would want to escape—and was pitch dark, which made it difficult to tell day from night. An amplified voice now made an announcement, but the girls couldn't catch the meaning. The door clunked open and two soldiers appeared. Bayonets leveled, they ordered the girls out.

The girls remained crouched for a moment, studying one another's faces in puzzlement, then realized they had to move. Outside, more than a hundred men were waiting. They flocked toward the girls and dragged them into the fields. The girls' silk *ch'ima* fluttered above the new shoots of grass.[13]

"How could they do such a thing with heaven above watching!"

Haha cooked a cauldron of barley and rice for rice balls. This was surprising enough, but then each girl was given two rice balls instead of the usual one.

"Eat up, girls. God knows how long we have left to live!"[14]

"Why do you say that?" Yŏngsun asked her.

"Why? Our Japan's about to be defeated by America. When she dies, we die and you die too."[15]

That evening an NCO staggered into the yard, smashed a bottle, stuck it in the ground, and drove his head onto it.[16]

7

S HE HAS DISAPPEARED from the edge of the veranda, where she sat just a few minutes ago. Her shoes snuggle up against each other as if wanting never to part company.

She's huddled off to the side of her bedroom. Before her are several newspaper clippings. She picks out one of them, about the size of a sheet of paper, and places it right in front of her. In the corner of the sun-yellowed newsprint a woman with a steely expression appears in a black-and-white wallet-size photo. Her eyes focus on the woman, whose name is Kim Haksun.

Kim Haksun . . . one evening she appeared on television, weeping like a faucet. She herself wept too, unable to swallow her mouthful of food. She couldn't contain her tears as the other woman cried.[1]

It was August 14, 1991—how could she forget? She was watching television by herself like on any other day and was astonished to learn of another living woman who had had the same exact experience as she.[2]

". . . I'm living proof, and I can't help weeping in despair when I hear such an outlandish denial that no such thing happened . . ."[3]

Which was why the woman had decided to summon the pool of reporters and let the world know of her experience.

The article is underlined here and there with red ink. Picking up the clipping, she reads the underlined areas. She doesn't read the sentences from start to finish but takes them in chunks, as if from a chopped-up frozen fish.

It's just me

No one to worry about

In such a harrowing life

God kept me alive till now

For this mission.

If I die, then that's that. Who would be interested in the miserable life of a woman like me . . .

Why couldn't I hold my head up like other people?

I am here to tell you that I am a victim![4]

Next came other comfort women, one by one, going public. "Me too, I'm a victim." "Me too, a victim." "Yes, me too, a victim." "Me too, I'm a victim." . . .

She heard on and off that the government had launched a program to register former comfort women. All one needed to do was report at a government office with a photo or other proof of identification, and once registered, the person would receive a living allowance.

She takes another clipping and reads it aloud, glancing at a black-and-white photo of an old woman.

"... *It was so difficult trying to make a living, so in 1993 I decided to register at the provincial office after hearing I would get assistance. Then someone from the office came to verify and confirm my experience. I hate talking about that stuff, it was really irritating, it upset my stomach, gave me a headache, and she interrogated me for hours: How many soldiers did I take? When the soldiers came in, how did they pull down their pants? Did I get syphilis?*

"*On she went, all that stuff I hated to talk about. . . . It was the worst interrogation, and I was going crazy. Was she having second thoughts? Or doubts about my past? Maybe so. But why on earth would I lie to her? Just for the sake of a government subsidy? . . .*

"*If I had a kid who could have helped out with my hospital bills I never would have thought of registering! I've lived my whole life hiding the truth . . . why should I spill everything at an age when I'm ready to croak. I blame it all on my unlucky fate, but now I'm mad at our government. What did I do wrong except being born poor and falling for the sweet lies of crooks?*

"*When I ran away from the comfort station I had syphilis. The pain I went through to cure that godawful disease! . . .*

"*This poor girl I know was able to get married, but when her husband came down with syphilis and her past came to light, he kicked her out. After that she gave birth to a boy, but at the age of forty he developed a brain disease. His doctor wanted to see the mother, so he called her in and*

*asked if she'd ever had syphilis. All she could do was weep in silence and
then she left. You see how evil that disease is? The poor woman—she never
meant to but she destroyed her son's life. He's no longer in a psychiatric
hospital but he has psychotic episodes. I doubt the doctor told him the
cause, but even so the son's been threatening to kill the mother, saying she
ruined his life by letting him into the world through that filthy hole of hers.*

"*Imagine how she felt! I take a daily aspirin but that day I took two
of them.*[5]

"*After registering, I felt lonelier. My sister tried to persuade me not to
register, she didn't want her kids' marriage prospects affected, and sure
enough, once I registered they stopped coming to see me.*[6]

"*I've been receiving government assistance since January of 1994.*"[7]

She can't fathom how those girls have lived so long suppressing their
past. Though she herself has kept mum the last seventy years.

Kim Haksun unleashed her confession after only fifty years.

She wanted to report along with Kim Haksun—*I'm a victim too!*
Whenever those words came to mind she'd find herself stuffing her
soft cotton hankie in her mouth.

*I'm a victim too . . . they took me to Harbin in Manchuria and made
me do godawful things . . . dirty things, and I was only 13 . . . just a baby.
. . .* These words shot up whenever she met her sisters but ended up
caught in her throat.

It seems only a few days ago that she heard 238 women had registered,
so how is it there's now only one left? As she shakes her head she hears
the ticking of the clock.

She looks up at the clock on the wall, with its round face and
dark hands.

There's no time.

The time it takes a bird to alight on a branch and take off—perhaps our life is that brief, eternal though it may seem?

※

Before she realizes it, there sits in front of her a sheet of paper instead of the newspaper clippings. In her right hand is a black marker.

She has never kept a diary or written a letter. How she wished to write home from Manchuria. But she knew neither her home address nor how to write, not even her name. Most of the girls at the comfort station were likewise illiterate. And knowing what she might have composed, she realizes how fortunate it is that she didn't.

> Hello Mother, hello Father, I'm here in Manchuria.
> Every morning the soldiers line up for me.
> Soon I'll be dead.[8]

Ignorant though she was, she worked briefly as a maid at a university president's home—until two weeks later, when her flustered gaze at the grocery shopping list gave her away and the wife fired her the following day.

She was well into her fifties when she learned how to read and write. She picked up a *hangŭl* primer at the stationery shop outside a grade school and began studying it. It took three months for her to be able to write her name. She's since copied it ten thousand times or more, but still she dithers and her hand trembles if she's called upon to do it.

Reading she can handle, but she's never felt comfortable writing.

ɪ

That's as much as she can manage. She caps the marker.

I?

What kind of person is she? She's not sure whether she's good or bad, cheerful or gloomy, headstrong or pliant, slow or brisk. Is she sad, cheerful, happy, crabby? The mistresses used to compliment her as a laconic, gentle maid while her sisters complained she was blunt and willful. Considering how chatty her sisters are, she doubts she was ever economical in her speech.

Whenever she thinks about herself, shame fires up first. It's humiliating and painful to remember who she is.

In the process of trying not to examine and reveal herself, she has forgotten who she is.

Her fingers briefly turn numb but then are charged with a burst of energy.

I'm a victim too.

What else should she write? She feels lost but realizes all too acutely that she hasn't forgotten a thing.[9]

She may not remember what she did an hour ago, but memories remain of the events of seventy years ago and earlier, down to the detail of how the light bulb flickered in her room in the comfort station.

She's heard that people criticize the comfort women for lacking credibility and being inconsistent because they have trouble remembering how old they were when they were taken away, who took them, and where they were taken. Why can't these people recognize that most of the girls didn't know the name of their ancestral village and without the benefit of education couldn't even write the three syllables of their name—how could they be expected to sort through decades of jumbled and fragmented memories?

She doesn't remember the name of the comfort station in Manchuria but can vividly recall Kisuk ŏnni dead from opium, her teeth glinting like pomegranate kernels from her own blood; the acidic, fishy smell of the gummy discharge in the *sakku;* and even the number of weevils sprinkled like black sesame seeds on the rice balls.

Sometimes, she remembers nothing except the cold and how severe it was.[10]

If I remember every last detail, then how could I live this long?[11]

Her experiences at the comfort station in Manchuria are like ice fragments scattered in her mind, each shard so cold and keen.

It's not easy to talk about stories kept silent for fifty, sixty, seventy years.

Just imagine, she couldn't even tell her own mother lying in her grave. Unable to unburden herself when she visited the grave, she could only pull at the new growth of grass before leaving.

She hates to remember life at the comfort station but is afraid that if she falls victim to dementia she won't be able to remember.

I'm a victim too.

8

SHE STANDS AT her bedroom window, face concealed by the mask, looking out impassively at the alley. "If I die, then that's that—who would be interested in the wretched life of a woman like me?" Her mumbling lingers between the mask and her face before dying out.

Her eyes see nothing because they're not aligned with the eye-holes, but she can visualize every nook and cranny in 15-*bŏnji*.

Younger sister number two, mother of five children, all living hectic lives, was on chemotherapy, and she was looking after her.

To her big sister, who had neither husband nor children, Number Two asked sympathetically, "*Ŏnni*, what do you want most?"

When her big sister didn't answer, Number Two said, "I want a gold ring, 23 karat, doesn't have to be too big, maybe two *ton* . . . one *ton* is too skimpy, three is too heavy . . ."

After Number Two fell asleep she told herself what she wanted most: *A mom. A mom is what I want most.*[1]

⁂

The broken bottle that the NCO planted upside down in the yard and then drove his head onto was still there. With the congealed blood it looked like a rusty crown.

Rumors circulated that Soviet soldiers were sweeping in and *otosan* would kill all the girls instead of leaving them behind.

"If we're gonna die this, that, or the other way, why not get out of here?" said Pokcha *ŏnni*.[2]

She herself made plans to escape with Pokcha *ŏnni* and three other girls—Kunja, Aesun, and a girl from Namhae whose name she couldn't remember. All the other girls wanted to join as well, but their swollen privates made walking difficult. Hyangsuk wept as she ushered them off.[3]

Pokcha *ŏnni*, her lice-infested hair covered with a black cotton cloth, took the lead and ran. She herself chased after; she was in such a hurry she'd put on a pair of mismatched *jikatabi*, rubber-soled socks.

The Namhae girl was shot by *otosan* as soon as she dropped from the far side of the barbed-wire fencing. Leaving her behind, the rest of the girls ran for their lives.

Their first hideout was an endless field of wild millet. The stalks were well over six feet high and swung incessantly. Pokcha *ŏnni*, who had promised not to cry, plopped down and broke into tears. Here and there they spotted low earthenware pots similar to soy-sauce crocks back home. Peering inside in hopes of finding something edible, she was hit with a potent stench. The Chinese had buried corpses inside the pots. Rain had seeped in and the smell of the rotting corpses ate away at her nose.[4]

They spent the night in the field with shafts of moonlight diffusing through the rustling millet leaves.

Before they knew it, the girls were separated from one another.[5]

Less than five days after their escape, she was on her own and found refuge in a Chinese home, the only habitable dwelling in sight. Spotting only men's clothing hanging from the collapsing earthen wall, she realized soon enough that a widower lived there. The man threatened to report her to the Japanese authorities if she left, and that would mean her death, so she was stuck there.[6] She wasn't aware that Japan had lost the war and Korea was liberated.

The man's supernatural instincts told him she was a runaway from one of those places they called a comfort station. He seemed to know what had gone on there.

For nine months she lived with the widower, who had lost all but three of his teeth, in the earthen hut with mice scurrying between her feet at meal time. The man worked at a distillery and constantly feared his new bride would run off and leave him. Several times she awakened at night petrified at the sight of him watching over her. The moonlight coming through the window gave his bony back the appearance of a washboard.

One day he came home toting a sack of sweet potatoes. She steamed them, leaves and all. He picked snails from the leaves and offered them to her.

She had never seen a hand as filthy and ugly. The viciously thrusting hand of the old kitten hunter in 15-*bŏnji* was not as horrifying.

But there was compassion in the widower's hand, dirty and hideous though it was.

When the dog at the alteration shop licked her hand, she thought of the widower's hand and wished the dog was licking that hand and not hers.

She lied to him that she would never, ever run away, that she would stay with him because he was a kind-hearted man. And when he put his worries aside, she ran.

In her wardrobe is a set of long underwear she has kept for the widower. She has a hunch that he is no longer of this world.

She wishes to see him if only in a dream, so she can tell him what she's kept in mind all these years.

You know I really wanted to stay with you since you were a kind man and treated me like your own daughter, but I missed my mother terribly ... I just wanted to see her face before I died ... I'm so sorry ...

❋

She sneaked out of the hut and walked off with no idea which way was which. Along the way she saw several men with pickaxes kill another man in a potato field.

Pickaxes dug into a person's back instead of the soil, axes chopped off heads, hands, and feet instead of tree limbs, and sickles cut into hearts instead of stalks.

A head severed by an axe fell to the ground and the eyeballs popped out and rolled free.[7]

She also saw charcoal black pigs gnawing on the charred face of a woman's corpse.

After the seething exodus of the Japanese soldiers, Soviet soldiers appeared. When they saw the girls, they took them into the fields—corn, millet, beans, or potatoes. Some of the girls managed to scramble away after the soldiers left, others never left.

She stole a dead boy's clothing to disguise herself and avoid being caught by the Soviets.[8] She felt as if she were stealing his soul. The boy looked like he was taking a nap and at any moment would get up, brush off his clothing, and continue on his way.

She also took a white *chŏgori* from a girl whose death had left her grimacing. Instead of wearing it she rolled it into a bundle and clutched it to her bosom.

Farther along she heard someone speaking Korean. "Please take me to Chosŏn," she begged the man.

A group of people seemingly blood-related agreed to do so, but not long afterward she found herself alone again.

A peddler told her he would guide her and not to worry, then took her into a cornfield. He ditched her among the tasseled ears of corn.[9]

She still can't figure out how she managed to reach the banks of the Tuman River on foot, penniless and directionally purblind as she was. And it's amazing she was able to avoid all the bombing of those past years.

Lacking a mental roadmap, she struck out toward hills where during the war Japanese soldiers had lit fires to flush out bandits.[10]

Past the charred hills she saw a rocky peak the color of lead. She arrived there after a day and a half to see people slinking down the nearly vertical slope. They lived at the foot of the mountain and came down to feed themselves on hidden staples under cover of darkness before climbing back up at daybreak. They were taking shelter from strangers who murdered innocent villagers and raped young women.[11]

If a girl looked in any way Korean, she rushed closer to scrutinize whether the girl was Pokcha *ŏnni*, Kunja, or Aesun.

She caught up with a girl whose slender waist reminded her of Kunja and found she was also a comfort woman. This girl was from Ch'ŏnan and learned about Korea's liberation after those who ran the comfort station disappeared.

"I heard the Soviet army would rush in and burn down the comfort stations," said the girl.

They walked together for three days straight. The refugees swelled into a human tide. Carried by the tide, the girl was beside her one moment but gone the next.

She saw an old woman plodding along with a hen held to her chest. Wondering if she was the woman in the white *ch'ima* and *chŏgori* at the Taegu train station with her hair in a bun and a hen held close, she went up to her but the old woman panicked and ran off screaming.

✼

The water whirled round and round,[12] reminding her of a rotating millstone. It was the Tuman River, people told her. After her five months' wandering from the Chinese widower's hut, the sight of the river turned her legs to jelly and she plopped down on the spot. The river was abysmally murky and turbid, and all she could think of was the river the girls had crossed on their way to the military outposts.

Her eyes followed Soviet soldiers moving on horseback and in trucks along the riverside, and she spotted corpses floating in the water. Bodies were also to be seen in the riverbank grass.

The Soviets were camped here and there, guarding the crossing of this river that formed the border between Manchuria and Chosŏn.[13]

She eavesdropped on whispered exchanges of information—which parts of the river were deep, which were shallow, where there were drop-offs in the riverbed.

People crossed the river at dusk, bundles kept dry on their heads.

Watching the swell of refugees, she burned with worries: what if she couldn't make the crossing that night?

A woman with a bundled infant on her back walked into the river. Instantly the water was up to the woman's waist. Her heart burned as she watched the river swallow them only to spit out the still bundled baby, and she heard the onlookers' laments: "Oh lord, they're going down!" "*Aigugu!*"

The swirling river sucked another woman under, her ink-colored skirt ballooning above the surface. *What happened to the woman and her baby? Did they make it?* She couldn't spot them.

A girl with a bulging belly was pulled under.[14]

Casting aside her dread and timidity, she clutched men's arms and pleaded, "*Ajŏsshi*, please help me across!"

No one offered a helping hand. What if they were sucked down trying to hold on to a girl so feeble she could barely stand? She stamped her feet in frustration as a group of girls slogged hand in hand through the water. She counted them, seven in all, and every single one made it safely to the other side.[15]

She followed the river upstream, searching for a narrower crossing she might be able to wade, and came across a sprawled-out woman who had been shot and killed.[16]

When the sun rose, fewer people attempted the crossing. A woman with a black head-towel walked toward the river hand in hand with a girl who couldn't have been more than 5. The woman sat the girl down at the side of the river and washed her face with the water through which the corpses were calmly drifting.

"*Ajŏsshi*, please help me across the river!" she begged a fortyish man.

The man wore knickers, a garment favored by *otosan*. "Hey, what have you got for me?"

"*Ajŏsshi*, are you married?"

"Married? Sure! A long time ago."

"*Ajŏsshi*, I have no money, only this nice *chŏgori*. Can I give you that?" She handed the rolled-up jacket to the man.

"My woman would fancy that!"[17]

The man took her wrist instead of her hand. She knew that in an emergency it would be easier for him to release her wrist.

9

THE OTHER SIDE of the river was home, or so she thought. She never expected it would take five more years to get the rest of the way there.

A month's walk brought her to P'yŏngyang Station, which bustled with passengers, job hunters, fortune-tellers, day laborers, beggars, and porters with back-racks. Her heart fluttered in anticipation of catching a train, and yet she was fearful.

Tagging after a rice-cake peddler, she begged him to take her somewhere she could work for meals.

The peddler considered her spotted, bony face and said, "Tell me, are you old enough to be having your period?"

"I'm over 20."

He found her a place behind the train station, an eatery serving hangover soup and drinks. It was run by a hunchback woman with a dogged belief that her son, who had been drafted into the Japanese army, would someday return home. She was saving up to buy a house for the two of them. She herself received three meals a day and clothing but no payment. She and the woman slept in the room attached to the back of the eatery. She needed money to get home, but dared not broach the subject.

A month after she started working there she related her story to an old laborer who came every night for the soup. Skipping the part about Manchuria, she told him she had gotten on the wrong train and ended up here in P'yŏngyang instead of Taegu and to make matters worse had lost the bundle with her traveling money and so she was stuck here and unable to go home.

"Then you should go sell yourself."[1]

Which she took to mean that he was going to send her back to the comfort station. And so that night she took a few notes from the money belt the hunchback woman had taken off before going to the toilet, and rushed to the train station. There she caught the train to the capital, Kyŏngsŏng, and transferred to another train that she assumed was bound for Taegu. When she got off she found herself in Pusan instead.

A granny with her hair parted down the middle, the part looking like a line drawn by chalk, was plodding along but kept glancing at her. Finally she approached.

"No place to go, little baby?"

She registered the old woman's use of *baby*.

"No."

"Why's that? Where'd you take the train, anyway?"

"I'm not sure—I can't read, you see." She couldn't bring herself to reveal that she'd been at the comfort station in Manchuria.

"You sure you don't have a place to go?"

"I swear."

"Then how about going to my place to babysit and do some errands?"

The place to which she followed the old woman was a Japanese-built bathhouse. She looked after a seven-month-old baby and ran errands but received no payment there either.[2]

Twelve years had passed, seven at the comfort station and five on the road. She didn't know the address of her home, only the name of the locality, Kkamakkol. She asked at the bus station how to get there. It was in a secluded area, requiring an hour-and-a-half bus ride from Taegu to the nearest town, and from there a thirty-minute ride on a bus that departed at two-hour intervals. On the local bus she could tell from the vibrations beneath her feet that the road the bus sped along like a mad bull was the same road taken by the truck that had made off with her and the other girls twelve years ago.

Standing where the bus had dropped her—she'd felt like a sack of potatoes as she stepped with a thud onto the ground—she put out feelers toward her village.

When finally she entered the yard she was greeted by a woman who turned out to be her new sister-in-law. Her mother had passed away, and her father was bedridden from a stroke. Younger sisters One and Two had been married off and the baby sister she had never met had left home to work in a factory that made fishcake. Brother and his family were the only ones left to take care of Father.

"Who are you?" inquired the sister-in-law as she emerged from the kitchen with a basin of dishwater.

That was the very question she herself wanted to ask the woman. She couldn't have dreamed that the woman with the mountainous belly carrying baby number four was her sister-in-law.

Without replying she looked around the house. It hadn't changed during her twelve-year absence, a tiny hole-in-the-wall dwelling[3] with a spiny orange tree that functioned as a hedge.

"Who are you?" came the question again.

Disheartened, she plopped herself onto the ground and wailed.

Father, though clear in the head, did not recognize her.[4] It had been a long time since he last saw her, and now her face was sallow and ruined like the wilted blossom of a rotten cucumber.[5]

As far as the family was concerned she was dead. Her brother had reported her as such after twelve years had gone by.[6]

The villagers who remembered her asked, "Where have you been all these years? You were a baby girl when you left."[7]

Most of them were first, second, or third cousins. An aunt, the wife of father's first cousin from Inner Kkamakkol, kept pinching her face as if she couldn't believe what she was seeing.

Even the sparrows, chickens, and goats seemed to be asking her, "Where have you been all these years? You were a baby girl when you left."

She fibbed that she had left home but ended up by mistake in Pusan, where she ended up working as a live-in maid.[8] She dared not tell them about Manchuria.

When dusk set in she stole out to her mother's grave to bawl. She never went near the river, afraid she would find the little 13-year-old girl still gathering snails.

One of her married cousins returned to the village for a visit and stopped by to see her. The cousin was the same age as she and had three kids by now.

Cooing to the baby strapped to her back, the cousin said, "You must have saved up some money working all these years as a maid."

"Sure. I used all my savings for some clothing and a new pair of shoes."[9]

The cousin brought the baby down from her back, undid her blouse, and put the baby to her breast.

At the home she'd longed to return to, if only as a spirit, she was merely an extra mouth to feed. Brother labored at the local mill and barely managed to provide for the family. Sister-in-law cooked watery barley gruel for them. Brother couldn't look her in the eye. Her baby sister saw her for the first time when she came to visit. She was standing under the persimmon tree, and her sister gazed at her, mystified. The two married sisters promised to visit but had yet to appear.

She hovered around the crock-pot stand passing her hand along the pots where her mother used to pray for her return.

She continued to stay away from the river.

One day she noticed a group of village men hurrying toward the river with a yellow dog. Its bloodshot eyes nagged at her memory. The dog that had made off with a dead boy at the Chinese village on the way to an outpost was yellow too.

A gamey roasting smell blew in from the river, reminding her of the smell of Tongsuk *ŏnni*'s burning corpse.

Sister-in-law returned from a visit to her family across the river. "The river's frozen over with thin ice."

She looked toward the river and saw on the bank a truck with a black rear flap. The truck with half a dozen girls in the cargo area also had a black flap. Twelve years ago she had flown through the air like a bird and landed among those girls.

"What's that truck doing over there?"

"What truck? I see only a cow."

"A cow?"

"Yes, Uncle Tŏksu's cow."

The cow looked like a truck to her. She went into the kitchen and came back out with a hoe and a basket.

"What're you going to pick?"

"Shepherd's purse."

"It's still winter, so maybe it's too early?"

She walked out into the rice paddy, trampling the old shoots, and after carving out the word *ttang*, "land," with the hoe, she looked up at the sky.

She left around the time that the new growth of shepherd's purse came poking out. One less mouth to feed was one less burden for her brother. Another cousin of hers, a live-in maid in Chinju, had visited just in time to recommend to her a banker's family there.[10]

On the way to the bus stop she encountered one of her aunties. "Where are you off to?" said the woman.

"I got a job as a maid."

"Are you going to live and die as a maid? A woman should get married and have kids."

It was her decision to leave, but she felt she was being taken once again to some alien place. Before setting out she had had her hair permed and secured with pins and she was now wearing a skirt and leather shoes.

She had returned home alive but legally was dead because none of her siblings was eager to correct her status in the official records, and she herself kept postponing action since the change in status was a time-consuming affair.[11]

Brother must have known. Unlike her bothersome sisters, Brother never brought up the subject of marriage. Having spent fall and winter at home after her twelve-year absence, she had informed him she was leaving to become a live-in maid again. "I'm just thankful you made it back home,"[12] he said.

Brother celebrated his eighty-first birthday then ended his life in a hemp field. He was discovered by the landowner face down in a furrow. A bottle of chemical fertilizer lay twenty steps away. Brother's fingernails were clotted with blood, attesting to his death agony.

She envisioned wild greens—shepherd's purse, wild garlic, and mugwort—bursting out of the ground as Brother consumed the fertilizer and began writhing. The combination of anticipation and horror was unsettling.

What had made him, octogenarian that he was, feel he couldn't bear to live another day and had to end his life?

What a heartless, driven man. This thought too occurred to her when she realized he hadn't let on even to his wife, her sister-in-law.

During an ancestral ritual this sister-in-law, oblivious to the end, nonchalantly mentioned that a distant relative had served as a comfort woman. "Can you believe she was wandering around in the snow without any shoes on? Her siblings had her committed to a mental hospital."[13]

Sister-in-law also mentioned that she had seen Kim Haksun on television, weeping. "And did you know that in Japan they say that the women in the Volunteer Corps went off to practice a trade?"[14] *Volunteer Corps?!*

"What trade?"

"Selling their body. You know that."

"She wouldn't have been crying on television if she'd gone off for that reason?"

"Well, I've heard even *kisaeng* want to make money."

She had known former *kisaeng* at the comfort station in Manchuria. Hyangsuk, member of a *kisaeng* union, had been led to believe she would be working in a high-class restaurant; never had she dreamed of serving a dozen or two soldiers a day in a comfort station.

"Why would any woman volunteer to serve in a living hell?"

"A living hell?"

"Yes, and what would possess a 12-year-old girl to do that?"

"You mean 12-year-old girls did that?" Gaping at her wide-eyed, her sister-in-law said, "They were too young to know better . . . they must have tagged along when the grownups sweet-talked them about making money."

Afraid her sister-in-law would catch on that she'd worked at a comfort station, she decided to keep her mouth shut.

Had Hyangsuk made it back home? Her Japanese name was Yuriko, the same name given to Kisuk *ŏnni*. Soon after Kisuk *ŏnni* died, *otosan* brought Hyangsuk to the comfort station. *Haha* said to her, "From now on you're Yuriko." *Haha* liked to bestow dead girls' names on the new girls, just like she would undress a dead girl and give the clothing to a new girl.

Countless soldiers went to war and didn't return or else returned injured, but the number of men who came to the girls never decreased, only increased. From where she lay Pokcha *ŏnni* could tell from which direction the men would swarm in. "They're coming from the east." And sure enough a locust-like swarm of men would arrive from that direction.

The Japanese soldiers thronged in from the south and from the east, north, and west as well. While the number of soldiers spiked by the hundreds and thousands, the number of girls increased by only seven, from thirty-two to thirty-nine.

The day after some seventy men[15] came and went from her body, she took her can of *sakku* to the washbasin and found Hyangsuk by herself also washing *sakku*. She kept her distance from Hyangsuk. Her privates throbbed and stung, as if she'd been mutilated with a knife. She felt like peeing, but not a drop came out. She counted the soldiers who had come and gone from her but gave up at sixty-eight.

Hyangsuk gave her a quick glance but she pretended not to notice. She kept her distance from Hyangsuk. Not that Hyangsuk was ever mean to her. But whenever she saw Hyangsuk, she associated her with Kisuk ŏnni. When *haha* and the soldiers called Hyangsuk Yuriko, she felt they were calling dead Kisuk ŏnni.

As she emptied her aluminum can of *sakku* and began to clean them, Hyangsuk said to her, "You didn't show up for breakfast. Couldn't you get up?"

She didn't respond.

"Takashi left some canned food with me. You can have it if you're hungry."

Takashi, one of Hyangsuk's regulars. Hyangsuk finished washing her *sakku* and approached her as she was putting her cleaned *sakku* back in her can. "You know, Takashi said he feels sorry for the Japanese guys too."

She couldn't understand why Hyangsuk would sympathize with the Japanese soldiers when she'd just washed the *sakku* they'd used.

"He said they were separated from their parents and siblings just like us and ended up here in Manchuria just to offer up their lives.

Yesterday I was missing my mom and crying and he said for me not to die . . . but do what I had to do to stay alive and return to Chosŏn and my mom."

During her seven years at the comfort station, thirty thousand Japanese soldiers came and went from her body. Of all those men, not a single one was kind enough to say, "Stay alive and make it back home."

※

Sitting against the wall with the window above, she fumbles with her black cell phone and flips it open. The screen is black as ink. She presses ON with her thumb and the screen brightens to a recorded melody.

She convinced herself she'd forgotten the number at her brother's home, but now it's come to mind. She enters the number.

At the same time she hears the *ding* that tells her someone has sent her a text message. And a second *ding*, and a third, and a fourth. She imagines the messages wandering the circuits of the phone when it's off.

Quickly she closes the phone. She leaves it off because of unknown callers. Her brother's family and her sisters are the only ones who know her phone number. A call from an unknown number terrorizes her, as if she's been flushed out from hiding.

She's disgusted whenever she mulls over the tribulations involved in reviving her citizen's registration. The day she received her new registration card she passed her hand over her chest, reckoning she could die that night—a dead body lacking an official registration card is a calamity, for it can't be buried or cremated.

The actual and official dates of her birth are different. As families were wont to do with female offspring, her father reported her birth a year after she was born. She's a November baby according to her registration card, but her mother knew she was born June 1 by the lunar calendar. Her mother remembered dawn spreading across the papered door to the room where she had given birth, barely able to collect herself afterward.

She's vexed at the thought that neglecting to report her new address may mean the expiration of the registration she reclaimed.

Yet again she feels all alone[16] and wishes she had a child, a daughter.[17]

When she was a live-in maid in Pusan she had a bachelor suitor. Despite the shuddering she felt at the thought of men, the prospect of a normal family life with this man prompted her to visit a gynecologist. The doctor said only that childbirth would be difficult because of her tilted uterus.[18] She dared not tell him about Manchuria, and without telling the bachelor she left Pusan.

Her menstruation stopped before she turned 40.[19]

Around that time she experienced swelling in her privates, which felt so heavy she thought they might separate from her. Such simple tasks as dishwashing became a chore, and she had to quit her job as a maid. When her nether regions were swollen, even bending or stretching her back was difficult. She tried all the "good-for-you" restoratives such as sweet pumpkin, carp, and Chinese herbal medicine, but to no avail. She massaged her lower abdomen with an ancient roof tile she'd heated, and that alone brought some relief. If a television show involved fighting or gunshots, she turned to a different channel. She didn't like people singing, she didn't like people who were loud, she didn't like people having fun—she didn't like anything.[20]

Hearing of a place in Hayang, Kyŏngsang Province, where women with "female problems" were treated, she dropped everything and went there for three months. From morning till evening you lay on a heated floor carpeted with a straw mat over pine needles and sea salt, with another straw mat on top of you. On the fifth day of this sauna-like procedure her skin began to come off and a yellow pus-like discharge oozed out.

Among the other women was one from Ulsan who might have been a comfort woman. She spoke with a Seoul or Kangwŏn Province accent, mixed with Japanese words, instead of the accent of her Kyŏngsang home. The woman related a lamentable story, saying she had gone to Japan as a girl to earn money but returned disabled, and though she looked fine there was no part of her that didn't hurt.

"I didn't do anything wrong, but I always feel like I did. I'll be going about my own business nice and quiet when out of the blue my heart starts hammering. Then I need a bowl of *makkŏlli* or else I'll croak. *Makkŏlli's* been my dinner for some time now. Once I was walking down the street pounding my chest and this woman at a fishcake factory comes up to me and says I've got a load of pent-up anger."

When she was a live-in maid for a family that had managed an herbal medicine shop for generations in Ich'on-dong in Seoul, the old herbalist read her fortune just for fun. He liked to check a patient's physiognomy and fortune while preparing medication. At the time she was well over 50 and mostly ran errands for the shop. One day he asked her the details of her birth—the day, the time, the phase of the moon, whether the sun was up. She told him she was born June 1 by the lunar calendar, around dawn. Translating that into 5:30 to 6:30 a.m., he said her fortune showed her to be an obstinate but truthful woman with a deep attachment to motherhood and a desire to raise a child with all her heart if one day her husband brought her a stepson.

Why then didn't she have children? she asked herself. If she was born with a deep attachment to motherhood, shouldn't she have at least one child to whom she should devote her motherly self? Wasn't there a correlation between motherhood and the blessing of having children? And if so, didn't that make childlessness a curse?

She was pregnant only once, at the comfort station and right after her first period. At the time she wasn't aware of it. At her weekly checkup a blob of blood came out of her after the injection from the doctor.

She still has a vivid image of the blood lump resembling a person.

When the bloody lump was released from her she felt her uterus had dropped out as well.

10

O N HER WAY BACK with tofu from the mini-mart she comes across an orange mesh bag hanging from the drainpipe of one of the homes. Inside the bag is a kitten. The pipe sticking out from beneath the home's slate roof is cracked and she fears it will break into smithereens if she touches it.

In the past two weeks she's counted six kittens inside bags. The old geezer has been nabbing every kitten he can get his hands on in 15-*bŏnji*.

She wonders if they're all from the same mother. This kitten is brown too, like the one she saw the day before in one of the alleys. And, coincidentally, like her Nabi, for whom she sets out food and water.

The bag hangs low enough for her to free the kitten. But she dares not.

❃

Gaze fixed on the television beyond the meal table, she stirs her bean-paste stew in its earthenware bowl. The rest of her dinner is thin-sliced tofu and kimchi with rice.

The television program shows a young African woman using flint and steel to light a fire of twigs. The woman is only 17 but a mother of three.

The young woman's 13-year-old sister, eyes round as jawbreakers, has come to stay with her. On her way home from school one day the girl was dragged into the woods and sexually assaulted by five rebels, leaving her with a severe hernia that required four operations, and she still has difficulty walking. In the town where the young woman was born and raised dozens of women, even those who are pregnant, are sexually assaulted. Government and rebel forces have been at war for decades, and the rebels assault the women to assert their power.

With a fear-ridden expression the younger sister standing at the door falters, "I don't know why they did that to me."

Those are precisely the words she would like to say but doesn't know how to. Astonished, she marvels that an African girl with a different skin tone could say this.

The scene changes and the girl is reading a book. She feels empathy when the girl says her dream is to become a teacher. What the girl experienced in the bushes on her way home from school seems no different from what the girls at the comfort station experienced.

She knows all too well how gruesome war can be. After four years of work as a live-in maid at the Pusan bathhouse, she was on her way back to her home village when the Korean War broke out.

Her memories of the war are inseparable from the image of the dead baby. Carried this way and that in the whirl of refugees, she happened to see two women abandoning a baby in a field. After the women hurried out and rejoined the flow of refugees, she went into the field and found the infant cold and dead. She crouched there holding the baby close, thinking it might return, bawling, to life. She followed the refugees with the baby to her chest, then came across a pumpkin field and all her senses came to life. The field was dotted with pumpkins huge as millstones and littered with soldiers killed by gunfire. Dyed a soiled red with the soldiers' splattered blood, the pumpkins looked like pork liver. She couldn't hold the baby indefinitely and finally she left it there.[1]

Suddenly the television goes dark. The fluorescent lights in her room and the veranda as well as the kitchen have gone out and the freezer has stopped running.

It all happened in an instant. She wonders if that's what will happen to her body in the end. Will she go blind and come to a stop all in an instant?

She was about to take a spoonful of stew but lays down her spoon and waits calmly until her ears are accustomed to the stillness and her eyes to the darkness.

She feels the world has come to end, and yet she's not afraid of the bleakness that envelops her like a walnut shell. As a child she believed the most frightening things were natural disasters that involved darkness, drought, or flooding. But after she turned 13 she learned the most frightening things are human beings.

She rummages through the drawer of the television stand and finds a candle and matches. She strikes a match by feel and touches it to the candlewick.

The tiny pepper-leaf-like flame flutters faintly, making her feel it's the last flame that will ever come alive for her.

Jumpy though she feels about the possibility of losing this last flame, she takes it through the recesses of her room and past the meal table and the dishes—the pickled sesame leaves, the earthenware pot, the spoon, the clear plastic water cup—and then along the window, her wardrobe, and the mirror and toward the ceiling.

She holds it toward the television and flinches—the paper mask looks just like a face.

The flame flickers and a thread of sooty smoke rises. The candle at the end of her outstretched right arm illuminates the fuse box. The circuit breakers, the wires in their black sheaths, and the meter come into view.

Sure enough, the circuit breakers are acting up. It's become frequent by now, and more often than not one of them will trip by itself. It's not a problem she tackles proactively, for she's still not knowledgeable about the workings of electricity. Her home village didn't have it when she was taken away at age 13. The notion that electricity runs not only through wires but through all sorts of other things intimidates her. She conjures up the various items that can conduct electricity—nails, coins, gold and silver rings, nickel silver pots, ladles, cast-iron caldrons, wires, chopsticks, water . . . people.

She did once consult with the meterman about the fuse box. His verdict was that the box might be too old and the whole thing ought to be replaced. Then he scared her by saying if the shit hit the fan an electrical fire might break out, leaving the house in ashes, and finally he suggested he could hook her up with an electrician he knew. She declined, feeling his kindness becoming burdensome, and in any event the matter needed to be discussed with her nephew. Besides, she figured the old man who collected wire could probably fix the circuit breaker without replacing the whole thing.

She climbs onto the chair she's positioned beneath the fuse box. Standing on tiptoe, she reaches for the circuit breaker.

❋

After doing the dishes she fills a pail with water and places it on the stove. Before it starts boiling she turns off the gas and transfers the hot water to the red plastic tub.

She secures the latch to the kitchen door.

Her ivory-colored blouse is already off, folded and placed next to the electric rice cooker. Next comes the pleated olive green skirt, which she likewise folds and then places atop the blouse. Socks off, she's down to the apricot-colored long-sleeve undershirt and loose rayon bloomers. She checks the door again. Now only her bra and panties remain. She unhooks her bra and steps out of her panties, covering her breasts as if someone is watching.

Even with the benefit of several layers of clothing, she sometimes feels she's standing naked in the middle of the street or lying on the cold ground with her privates exposed.

She steps into the tub and sits with her knees to her chest. The water ripples and rises all the way to the brim.

Her senses and her body don't work very well together, she feels.

She cups water and splashes it over her shoulders. The water feels silky compared with the water in Manchuria. How she longed for the water at home when she was at the comfort station in Manchuria. She used to believe water was the same everywhere, but her hair became stiff as twigs when she washed it in the Manchurian water.[2]

She washes her privates with salt water. For ten years after her return the itching down below drove her crazy. If she was out and about she would have to jump into a secluded alley to scratch.[3] At home, while rinsing rice or doing laundry in the yard, she would have to escape to the toilet, where she scratched until her panties were stained with

blood. Peeing made her feel like bees were stinging her.[4] At night, mas-
saging herself with hot water lulled her to sleep. If her privates were
fingers she would have lopped them off long ago.

Drying herself down below with a towel, she flinches as a bead of
water drops onto her sparse pubic hair, reminding her of a crab louse.
As much as she's washed, she still feels unclean.

Kim Haksun said her husband used to call her a dirty bitch in the
presence of her child.

She changes into clean clothing, all of it white. She changes her underwear daily and her outerwear every three or four days. She trims her
nails attentively and brushes her teeth after every meal, because of
her obsession over suddenly dropping dead and being found by a
trespasser. She wants her dead body to look neat and clean, and the
stranger not to feel soiled when he touches her.

If at all possible she would like to meet death here in this house,
drawing her last breath in the presence of the furniture and other items
she has used.

How many people meet death in their home? When she was
younger she expected that only animals would die away from their
home. But people are no different from animals. Her three sisters died
away from home, one at a hospital and the others at a nursing home.

She wonders who would discover her body. Her nephew? Better a
total stranger.

It's after midnight when one of the television stations shows photo
clips of the last surviving comfort woman. The photos along with the
melancholy music are a replay of a feature aired more than ten years
ago. When the girls dwindled to forty survivors, the television stations
began broadcasting daily reports about the comfort women, using the

photos to detail the everyday life of one of the women. She herself was living in Ŭijŏngbu at the time, doing piecework where she lived, and she took to leaving the television on twenty-four hours a day. The mere mention of comfort women had her head jerking up toward the screen as she attached labels to necklaces. She held her breath as the women testified to their experiences at the comfort stations. They were telling the story she had never dared tell a soul.

She never missed this feature, her curiosity aroused by the life stories of these women with whom she had coexisted.

She's disappointed that it's a rerun. She's curious as to how the last one lives now, where and with whom, and if she's mobile.

What's more, this rerun is coming on too late at night. Still, without realizing it, she's sitting closer to the television.

So she lives by herself, just like I do. The camera shows the living room, the kitchen, and the room where she sleeps. It's a small apartment but it doesn't look needy. Everything seems to be in place. The baby green curtain in the living room flutters dreamily.

The camera captures the last one sitting on a brown fabric sofa. She wears green slippers and a mustard-colored sweater over gray pants. She's slender and sits upright. Her face looks like a face in a passport photo. She has well-defined features and a long groove beneath her nose. She's a gutsy-looking woman. Her salt-and-pepper hair is pulled back, making her forehead all the wider and more handsome.

"I like flowers,"[5] the last one says. There's an array of yellow mums and orchids beneath her living room window. She caresses the mums as if they're babies, the flowers seeming to shudder at her touch.

"And not just flowers—I like dramas, dogs, cats, rice cake, red-bean gruel, coffee too. Can you guess why I have so many things I like? I just don't think about what I don't like."

The last one gets up and goes into her kitchen. She peels a peach she's just washed.

"A person shouldn't live without a purpose, not even for a day. Those flowers are there for a purpose. I water them so they won't die and so they'll bloom when they're supposed to. I need to get up, keep my energy up, and get myself busy, just to water them."

She lives alone but keeps to her mealtimes, and she always sets the table, even if the meal is only a single dish.

On the table is a pot with a tiny cactus.

"Isn't it a miracle that a flower blooms inside all those needles?"

The cactus looks like an upside-down bowl in the middle of which an orange blossom is besieged by spines.

"Sweet but worrisome . . . that flower is just like me."

The interviewer, who looks barely 30, is seated across from the last one. Cautiously she asks why the last one has never married.

"I was born from the purest mother, but I got ruined over there. How could I marry anyone? I wouldn't want to ruin that person. I would have to deceive him, and how could I live with that. . . . I had this disease, a terrible disease, they say I'm cured but it still makes me itch, spring and fall."[6]

The last one forks a peach slice into her mouth. "Mmm . . . so sweet. Now if you can hold the questions and just listen . . ."

The last one made a living running a small eatery.

"Nobody knew a damn thing. And then the girls started registering, the news came out on TV, and people got to know. Until then everyone was in the dark—but of course the news would have been so appalling. Once the words 'comfort woman' began circulating, friends and acquaintances kept their distance from me. It wasn't the same anymore, so I shut down my little restaurant.[7] The ones who kept in contact and stayed with me, they're my real friends."[8]

The last one's greatest joy is reading. She got hooked on a world literature series a neighbor discarded when moving. She never made it to grade school but taught herself *hangŭl* at age 30.

The last one gets up from the table, goes to the room where she sleeps, and returns with a book. "*Resurrection*; it's by a Russian writer. I'm reading it for the sixth time." She settles herself on the brown sofa. Retrieving a magnifying glass from the corner table, she reads in a soft voice from the very beginning of the novel. And then, transferring her gaze to the interviewer, she says, "How miraculous that the shoots spring up and the birds do their nesting even after hundreds of thousands of people tried their best to turn that small parcel of land into a wasteland. You can't imagine how I cried when I read that for the first time. I don't cry usually . . ."

Grinning at the interviewer, the last one resumes reading, from a passage that emphasizes the happiness of all living things and the God-given beauty of the world.

At night she herself is alone. She will slip beneath a quilt that is gorgeously embroidered with plum-colored flowers in full bloom. Like every other night, although she leaves her lamp on as if for a guest, no one will tiptoe in and slide in next to her.

·⁂·

Before laying out her sleeping pad, she wipes down the floor with a rag. But before she eases herself beneath the quilt, she has to check the veranda.

She kneels before the sliding door to the veranda. The panes of glass tremble.

She slides open the door and the cool air jumps into her bosom like a frisky child. She reaches down to the shoe ledge and retrieves her shoes.

She scans the veranda then hides the shoes behind the trash can—if Nabi can't find her shoes maybe it won't leave her a dead magpie.

Now she can lie down, but sleep won't come easily. Turning down the alteration shop woman's offer of the dog bothers her: what's the woman going to do with the dog now that it's too feeble and old to bear puppies? It doesn't seem right that the fate of a dog depends on a person.

※

Ever since she began keeping her shoes out on the veranda at night, Nabi has brought no gifts. Nor has she had visitors—no nephew, no one to read the electricity, no one to read the water meter. She waits for no one but feels uneasy having no visitors.

11

S HE RUSHES OUT from the kitchen, where she's been doing the dishes. It must be her nephew. But no, it's a man from the city offices who looks about the same age as her nephew. He wears a navy blue windbreaker and charcoal gray trousers and holds a file folder. His black shoes practically glitter.

He explains that he's trying to determine who the actual residents of 15-bŏnji are.

"Actual residents?"

"Yes, not the fake ones, but the people who actually live here."

She doesn't get it. Are there fake residents? What's a fake resident anyway?

"Some people report that they live here then go live somewhere else. They say they live here so they can get priority rights to a new apartment, but they don't actually live here. It's a royal headache."

She's reminded of the peculiar rumor she heard from the alteration woman a couple of days ago: the city and the district can't agree on the redevelopment plan for 15-*bŏnji* and so it's been canceled. And now that the redevelopment plan that's straggled on for seven years has gone up in smoke, the landowners have formed an association in order to privatize the project. She slept fitfully that night wondering what will happen with the lease-to-own rights for a new apartment.

"Do you live alone?" the man asks as he looks about the Western-style house.

"No ... my nephew lives here," she answers, in accordance with her nephew's instructions.

"Your nephew."

"Yes, and his wife . . . I don't live here," she says with a *no-no-no* wave of the hand for emphasis. And then adds that they're off visiting their daughter, who got married and moved to Shanghai, and she is housesitting for them. Knowing that she's fibbing makes it impossible to look the man in the eye.

"Can't leave the house empty ... so—"

"Then where do you live, ma'am?"

"In Pusan," she mumbles in spite of herself.

"Pusan? Where in Pusan? That's where my wife's from, so I know my way around there."

"... in Pusan."

"Pusan is a huge city—where in Pusan?"

"Near Chin Market ..." The bathhouse where she worked as a maid was near the market.

"Ah, the market! I've been by there several times—my wife's home isn't very far. . . . So when are your nephew and his wife returning?"

"When?"

"Yes, you said they're visiting their daughter."

"About ... two weeks from now?"

He opens the folder and jots down something.

"What is it you're writing?"

"Oh, nothing much."

"But . . ."

"So you're going back down to Pusan when the nephew and his wife return?"

". . . I assume so."

She closes the gate behind him and turns back toward the kitchen but stays where she is, inspecting the house as if she's never seen it before. It's not her house, but she lives here. It's not the house where she was born, but maybe it's the house where she'll die.

Morning and evening she sweeps, wipes down, and tends to the house just like she tends to her body, but she makes sure to leave no trace of her life here, not even a nail hole.

※

Afraid the man from the city might return, she doesn't want to remain in the yard.

She brings her shoes in, slides shut the door to the veranda, and stays inside. Maybe that way people will think no one lives here.

She's also concerned that her nephew hasn't stopped by for well over a month. Deep down inside she's worried that something has happened to him. If he won't get priority on a new lease-to-own apartment, he has no reason to renew the lease on this house. She wonders if she should look for a place of her own. And if she finds one, then how would she go about reporting it?

Before living in Ŭijŏngbu she occupied a leased multi-housing unit in the city of Suwŏn. There were six other families in the building, which was collateral on a loan taken out by the landlord, who ultimately vanished, and the building ended up being auctioned off. She had hoped to salvage her 30-million-*wŏn* security deposit but was dismayed to learn that she alone among the tenants had been excluded from receiving payments following the auction. The other tenants were too engrossed in retrieving their own security deposits to inform her. She believes the other tenants wouldn't have shown her such disrespect if she weren't an aged single woman. Even though she kept a low profile, they must have had an inkling that she was a single woman with neither child nor husband.

Her wish is to live and die quietly without troubling anyone and without being treated with disrespect.[1]

Taking out her black cash bag and sliding the drawer shut, she unzips the bag and lays out its contents—bankbook, wooden stamp, national ID card, a roll of cash amounting to 10,000 *wŏn*, and a jade ring.

She inspects each and every one as if it's an unclaimed lost-and-found item.

She leafs through the bankbook—the first page, the second, the third, and the fourth. How incredible that all her savings are recorded in those pages! She's never gotten used to the saddening notion that money is the only thing she can depend on.

She's well aware of how much she's saved, but she's forever checking to make sure it's all there, a little more than 20 million *wŏn*. She wouldn't feel so high and dry if she'd managed to recover that 30-million-*wŏn* security deposit. And if her sister had returned the money she'd borrowed. . . . In an emergency her sisters would borrow money from her—after all she must have socked away some cash working as a live-in maid and having no one to take care of. Were they unaware she could no longer draw interest if she withdrew her savings prematurely? Did they know she was able to save by not splurging on nice overcoats and fancy face cream?

After she turned 60 no one was eager to take her in as a maid. Restaurants felt she would be a burden. And that's when she moved to Ŭijŏngbu and did piecework attaching labels to necklaces. Having to crouch over her work all day left her with indigestion and her fingers so cramped she could barely spoon herself soup and rice.

She knows her savings will outlast her time on this earth, but still she uses it as sparingly as possible. The Creator knows how long she will live, but while she's alive she has to have money. If her nephew decides to cancel the lease, the first thing she'll have to do is find a place to rent.

Whenever the former comfort women appeared on television she became curious about how they managed—even though the knowledge was vexing and disturbed her sleep. There was little in the way of work they hadn't tried, but still they weren't able to get a decent home to lease,[2] or they barely eked out a living even with government assistance,[3] or they made ends meet with part-time work.[4]

The former comfort women have found work as live-in maids, like her, at eateries, or as peddlers. She knows that some of them, despairing over their ruined lives, ended up at brothels.

Too anxious to stay home, she skips lunch and leaves. But she feels nervous wandering the alleys—what if she runs into the man from the city?

She comes across a wide-open gate. The yard inside is strewn with discarded furniture. Approaching the gate, she takes the rusty, corroded handle to pull it shut. The gate closes with a screech but opens again as soon as she releases it. She tries once more to close it tight. Knowing it will open again, she keeps hold of the handle.

She won't walk past a home, even a vacant one, if the gate's been left open. She has to close it first. She's a firm believer that a house has a soul. To her the ambiance, warmth, and smell of the house are its spirit. Some spirits shine, some are serene, some are lonely, and some are dejected.

Whenever she closes the gate to a vacant home she feels she's left a house in which she's lived her entire life.

"*Halmŏni.*" She turns toward the voice thinking perhaps she's misheard.

A man is smiling at her. The meterman.

"*Halmŏni*, what are you doing out here?"

She just looks at him.

"I mean, why are you here?" Sounding to her like *You shouldn't be here*. "Did you lose your way home?"

"Home?"

"Yes, home!"

She shakes her head no.

"Your place is over there." He points over her shoulder.

". . . over there?"

"Yes, over there!"

She doesn't respond.

"Did you forget? Would you like me to take you there?"

How would it be possible for him to know where I live but not me? She decides to keep her mouth shut.

The unexpected run-in with the meterman leaves her feeling driven as she continues through the alleys. Something drops in front of her. She jerks her head up to see a dove hovering on a slate roof. Then looks down to see an egg at her feet. Examining the cracked white shell and the ruptured yellow yolk, her eyes grow tranquil like the surface of a lake. Did the egg fall by itself? Or did the dove push it?

❀

The man from the city must have stopped by the alteration shop. The woman will know what's going on.

Dog held under her arm, the woman welcomes her while munching on a kimchi pancake. The woman has told her she takes a pill for her diabetes, but she's always munching on something.

"A man from the city is going around the neighborhood . . ."

"From the city?"

"Yes, checking on . . ."

"Checking on what?"

"On the status of the actual residents . . ."

"Oh *that*. I can't believe it. The city and the district cozy up to each other and drive out the longtime residents, and now they're looking to privatize the project to save money. What the hell do they think they're doing?"

Agitated, the woman sets her dog down. It crouches there motionless, like a still life.

Without realizing it she reaches for the dog and strokes it. "Poor thing," she murmurs, as if she's talking in her sleep.

"Poor thing?" the woman snaps.

"Yes, fifty puppies coming out of this little thing."

"It's people you need to feel sorry for, not a dog."

"People?"

"Yes! Think about it. You work yourself to death, raise kids, get them married off—it's endless. And what thanks do we get? When the parents get old, what do the kids do? They dump them in a nursing home, standard procedure."

Just then they spot the old man and his son passing by the sliding door to the shop. Eyes fixed on them, the woman mumbles, "I don't know why, but a few days ago he was banging his head against the wall . . ."

"Who was?"

"The son! No matter how the old man tried to stop him, he wouldn't calm down, just kept banging his head till he was bleeding. You know, that idiot is stubborn as a mule. So the old man follows him everywhere, even to the pot. He ditched him once, you know."

"What? Ditched him?"

"Yes, maybe thirty years ago . . . he got drunk out of his mind and was going around the neighborhood wailing and screaming that his kid had gone missing. Well, all the neighbors were suspicious, they figured he must have dumped the kid somewhere. I mean, someone saw the two of them leaving home first thing in the morning. Can you imagine what it's like for a widower to have to live with a dumb kid?"

What if it was me? Would I have believed him? Or would I have been suspicious like the others?

"The old man was living with a woman who was ten years younger, and one day he comes home from work and finds she's locked up the boy and run off—and the kid was still shitting in his pants. She must have wanted more out of life than getting old and broken down. I mean . . . old husband and idiot son . . . she must have figured sooner is better. Anyway, three or four months later, what do you know, the old man shows up with the kid. You should have heard the neighbors yapping . . . some were sure he brought the kid back out of guilt, some thought he really had lost the boy . . ."

"You mean he dumped his own son . . ."

"Sure, why not? But then he must have gone on a guilt trip and brought him back . . . don't underestimate what people are capable of."

"Yes, people . . ." She can only nod, over and over. Yes, it was people who took her away when she was barely 13. One moment she was at home, the next moment she'd been dumped in Manchuria.

The orange mesh bag is swaying from a gray metal gatepost. Something's not right—the bag wouldn't be swaying if a kitten were inside.

She hesitates, then steps closer and looks inside the bag. Empty. Someone has set it free. Who could it be? Who would want to free it?

❈

With the blue wrap around her neck she looks into the mirror. She couldn't refuse the Seoul Beauty Shop woman's offer to color her hair. While the woman is on the phone she stares at herself in the mirror. The blue wrap makes her look like a stuffed bird mounted on a wall, especially with her feet dangling in midair from the high seat.

The beautician ends the call and returns with the colorant.

She stopped coloring her hair when she turned 80. Women want to look younger, it doesn't matter how much, but not her. Women dream of returning to their maiden days, but not her. At the height of her youth she wanted to age quickly.

"Michiko?"

"Yes . . ."

Her closed eyes open toward the mirror.

"Who's Michiko? You kept saying Michiko, Michiko."

"Did I really?" Her eyes open wide in response to the beautician.

"Yes, maybe half a dozen times!"

She doesn't remember. That she called out that name in her drowsy state makes her shudder.

"Who is she anyway? You were calling her like a mother who misses the daughter she's married off." The woman's hands are busy as she applies the colorant, but her face in the mirror is suspicious.

"Someone I used to know a long time ago," she reluctantly explains, her eyes constantly moving.

"How long is a long time ago?"

"More than seventy years . . ."

"More than seventy years ago—which would make it . . . oh my god!"

"She died young, she had a terrible disease . . ."

While she was trying to process the meaning of "bedding with soldiers," *haha* had told her, "From now on your name is Michiko."

Hair washed, she returns to the chair in front of the mirror. Her new ink-black hair color and dry orange skin tone are a total mismatch.

She resents the beautician for coaxing her into coloring her hair, and at the same time pities her. The woman had a mastectomy and has regular check-ups at a clinic an hour distant by subway. Keeping her shop open for permanents and hair coloring seems intended to showcase how repulsive she feels about having to continue to make a living. The woman brags that her clientele goes back decades and the women still come to her even though they've moved out of 15-*bŏnji*. But she herself suspects there are days when the woman has no customers.

The woman drapes the blue wrap over her again and picks up a pair of scissors.

"Just a little trim!"

Before she can say yes or no the woman starts snipping. It's not a trim but a cut. The nape of her neck feels bare.

Her face staring into the mirror grimaces. At the comfort station in Manchuria her hair was always dark, short, and bobbed, just like now.

While the woman is in the bathroom she places 5,000 *wŏn* on the table and leaves.

❉

The mini-mart man is out somewhere, leaving the woman to mind the shop. From the room in back of the shop she's lying on her side facing out toward the shop while she watches television. Her disheveled hair looks like a wig. Pumped-up cackling and applause come from the television.

She takes one of the black plastic bags from their holder and packs the eggs she's buying. *What if I get so old and weak I can't even buy an egg?* The notion frightens her. If only she can wash, cook, and dress herself till the very end.

"Here's for the eggs." Taking three 1,000-*wŏn* bills from her wallet, she sets them within reach of the woman, who fumbles for change in her safe before dropping a half dozen 100-*wŏn* coins at the door sill. The coins roll every which way, one of them coming to rest beside the woman's bushy hair.

She's about to reach for that coin but thinks better of it, gathers the others, and leaves.

Walking up the alley with her eggs, she stops in front of the *hanok* to catch her breath. She remembers that she once found the gate to this traditional house open and had to close it.

She checks the alley to make sure no one is watching, then opens the gate and goes to the dust-layered veranda. Perching herself on the corner, she surveys the weed-grown yard.

After a time she takes an egg from the bag and sets it on the veranda. She takes another egg and places it next to the first one. And then a third egg. Like a hen that's found a hidden spot to lay. And then she leaves.

Where she sat on the veranda is a round trace of her presence, looking like a circle made by an eraser.

※

In the dim, shaded alley she comes across a dead kitten slouched on the paved surface, looking like a wad of gum that's been spit out after the flavor is gone. She wonders if it was sick or if it starved to death. And of course this one, too, is brown.

She walks on by, pretending not to see the dead kitten, just like she'll pass by a mesh bag with a live kitten as if she hasn't noticed it.

But at the end of the alley she makes a round trip back and squats next to the kitten. Setting down the bag of eggs, she takes from her skirt pocket a white hankie embroidered in one corner with violet forget-me-nots. It's one of the first items she ever bought, years ago, a cherished belonging that has never touched her nose. She wraps the kitten inside it.

If there is a Creator, she would pray to it to take the kitten to a happy place.

Her baby sister used to have a grocery list of prayers covering everything from her grandson's studies to her chain-smoking husband's addiction to nicotine.

If there's one prayer she could offer up for herself, it would be a return to the riverside in her home village back when she was 13.

She greeted with scorn the news that man had set foot on the moon. As much as science had advanced, it couldn't take her back to the riverside. The river of her home village was much more distant than the moon.

※

The old man's yard is so littered with wire there's no place to step. She's arrived at his place without really thinking about it. The wall is a crumbled mess that leaves the entire yard in plain sight. The old man's back is to her as he hunkers down stripping the copper from rolls of wire. Some of the wire is thin as an earthworm, some is thick as an eel.

Slicing off the cloth coating and ripping out the copper looks daunting. Securing a roll of wire with his left foot, he makes a long slit along the cloth coating as if gutting an eel. Then he peels the cloth apart and with pliers pulls the copper free.

He stuffs the copper into a sack, and the cloth strips go into a pile at his feet. He takes another clump of wire and repeats the process.

Casing an empty house, locating the electric line, opening the interior walls to rip out the wiring, bagging the wire and taking it home, stripping the cloth and pulling out the copper—harvesting copper from abandoned homes is serious business.

Turning away, she is startled by the son, who is smiling from ear to ear. She hurries off.

Beyond the crumbling wall she has an eerie feeling and looks back. The son is following her, and his smile has become a ludicrous smirk.

"Do you know me?" she asks him, wishing she was asking the Creator instead.

If there are ten thousand bees in a hive, does the Creator know each and every one of them? Even if so, the Creator couldn't possibly know her.

"Do you . . . do you know me?" she repeats.

The son nods.

She turns away from him feeling in her heart that she is shunning the Creator.

12

A HUMID BREEZE LEAVES her hair strewn and her nose full of the chemical in her hair colorant. Alone in the alley, she wonders if the son has made it home safely.

She wonders what will happen when the old man is gone. Who will feed, dress, and bathe the son?

❊

Mother dying... Mother dead.

These telegrams had been posted a month apart, but Punsŏn received them at the same time. She didn't reply to them and never again sent a telegram home.

Punsŏn was taken away by the Japanese MPs at the age of 14 while she and her mother were picking cotton.

"Don't you take my little girl, you'll have to kill me first!"[1] her mother screamed as she clutched Punsŏn. The MPs stomped on her belly.

Punsŏn said she could never forget the image of her mother writhing and screaming in the cotton field.

When Ch'unhŭi ŏnni became lucid again she didn't realize that some of the girls had left the comfort station during her illness.

"I don't see Punsŏn, where is she?"

"You know, she went home—her mom died," Pongae told her.

"What about Haegŭm?"

"She went to work in a silk factory," Pokcha ŏnni chimed in.

Haha approached the girls in her click-clacking geta.

"Heaven will punish that bitch," Ch'unhŭi ŏnni said as if chanting a spell.

When she was 17 she dreamed she had lost a tooth. A front tooth. There was no bleeding, though. She awoke with a jolt and found an old soldier, a captain, sleeping next to her.

"A family member must've died." Pokcha ŏnni, so accurate in forecasting the soldiers' movements, offered this interpretation of her dream, a service she performed for the other girls as well.

"Who could it be?"

"I wonder who . . ."

By the time she was 26 Pokcha ŏnni had no teeth left.

Her own paternal grandparents had passed on before she was born. Her father said that her grandmother had starved to death.

The girls longed for their family, even in their dreams. At the same time they thought it a bad omen, an indicator of misfortune, illness, or death, if a family member appeared in a dream.

In tears she sought out Hyangsuk, finding her in her room with a bowl of hair-colorant sitting before her. She guessed Hyangsuk wanted to kill herself.

"But I just can't do it. Mom keeps saying no. She used to tell us it was unfilial for a kid to die before her parents. She had nine kids in all, and four of them died—two right after they were born and another one when he was two. And then I had a brother, three years older than me, who was learning *judo*, and he got typhoid fever and died. He wanted to be a constable, and a constable has to be skilled at *judo*. He worked with a pull cart during the day and went to *judo* school at night. He always said Japanese dogs were better off than Koreans. The Japanese feed rice to their dogs and pig swill to Koreans. If he'd been a constable, I wouldn't have ended up here. He wouldn't send his sister or daughter to a hell like this, right?"

It was around Ch'usŏk, the harvest-moon festival. When Ch'usŏk drew near—and the girls felt it instinctively even without a calendar to go by—they were beside themselves with thoughts of home.

Four days of horrid rain came to an end and a truck from an outpost was sent for the girls. Six girls climbed into the cargo bed— she herself along with Pongae, Sundŏk, Miok ŏnni, Yŏngsun, and Hanok ŏnni. It was the first time for Pongae. Hyangsuk was supposed to go but her broken arm hadn't mended and she was replaced by Pongae.

Hyangsuk had been asking about Takashi, who hadn't visited her for some time, but there was no news of him. He must have been killed in battle, the girls whispered. A drunken Japanese soldier found her sobbing in bed and grew livid—a *Chosen ppi* who was crying and ignoring the soldiers was bad luck. When Hyangsuk continued to cry he hit her so hard he broke her arm.

The road was soggy and clumps of mud the size of cattle dung spattered the girls, faces and all.

After a half day's travel the truck arrived at a river. A ferry shaped like a clog was waiting. The four days of rain had left the river frightfully swollen. The turbid, muddy water scared her and yet it would be nice to be out of the truck.

The girls clambered out and hopped onto the ferry, along with the soldiers. As soon as the girls were hunched down at the bottom of the vessel, the Chinese ferryman, whose bald head gave him the appearance of a boiled octopus, set to work with his oars. He had stripped to the waist and his sun-darkened skin was the color of ink.

The motion of the ferry was uncomfortable, but strangely enough she entered a state of utter peace, as if her life had run its course. If only the ferry could go on and on to a place where she and the other girls would arrive as wrinkled old grannies.

Pongae pointed and said to the girls with a sigh, "Look, a village..." Her pockmarked face was sallow and lumpy like bean-curd dregs.

Squinting because of the headwind streaming along the river, she looked to where Pongae was pointing. The village looked far off and at the same time within arm's reach. Everything looked red and had a fuzzy, dreamlike quality.

"I don't think anyone lives there..."

"How could that be?"

"I don't see a soul."

"Maybe they're all sleeping."

"A few days ago I dreamed I was back home. But no one was there—father, mother, my brothers and sisters . . . I was just walking around with a dead baby on my back—"

And the next moment Pongae rose like a ghost and jumped into the river. She shot out a hand to grab Pongae's skirt but by then Pongae was gone. A split-second later the girls were calling her name, but it was too late. She screeched until she smelled blood in her throat, but Pongae didn't surface. The ferryman had stopped rowing and was shaking his head as if to say it was no use.

The soldiers leveled their rifles at the agitated girls and the ferry-man resumed rowing as if nothing had happened.

Not until their return trip to the comfort station did the girls see Pongae again. They were sprawled awkwardly across the floor of the ferry, their eyes hollow, their privates swollen, and their hips strained from five straight days of taking soldiers at the outpost.

"Isn't that Pongae?" Hanok *ŏnni* blurted.

"*Aigu!* Yes, it's Pongae!"

Her body had been snagged by a branch of an uprooted tree that was upside down in the river. Pongae's face was above water and she seemed to glare at the girls as if she'd been waiting all this time for them to rescue her. Her waterlogged stomach was bulging.

At the request of the girls the soldiers pulled Pongae onto the ferry. Arriving at the riverside, the girls gathered twigs into a kind of bed and lay her down on it.

Sundŏk wiped down Pongae's sodden face, which was chafed and scraped and looked like rats had gnawed on it. But Sundŏk, tearful though she was, didn't seem the least bit scared or reluctant to do so.

The soldiers sprinkled gasoline over the twigs and lit a fire and in no time flames were soaring aloft. Leaving the flaming corpse, the girls climbed into the back of the truck. Sparks shot up like a tapestry of fireflies. She reached for the sparks as if they were Pongae's soul, but in her grasp they were dark and lifeless.

She blamed herself for Pongae's death. If only she'd reached out more quickly to grab her skirt . . .

She always blamed herself when a girl at the comfort station died.

※

As always she turns on the television first thing in the morning. No news about the last one. Good—there is still one left.

Folding her blanket, she spews out a deep breath at the realization that the last one doesn't have much time left—whether the last one is she herself, the woman she sees on television, or someone elsewhere.

She sticks a foot beneath the veranda for her shoes and flinches. A magpie. Nabi must have come by, but when? There's no sign of the cat in the yard.

She feels that the magpie—like Hunam ŏnni, after otosan took her from her room and dumped her out on the wasteland—still retains a breath of life.

She slides a pair of fingers beneath one of the wings and feels a touch of warmth that reminds her of living breath. Cupping the bird in her hands, she sets out for the alteration shop. The woman there can tell if the magpie is still alive.

The woman is having breakfast at the low round table in front of her television. The table contains an array of side dishes. The television is loud enough for passersby to hear. As the woman opens up a grilled croaker fish with her fingers she turns toward her guest.

"What have you got there?"

Nervously she holds out the magpie.

The woman shudders. "Oh my god, that's a *magpie*."

"Can you tell if it's still breathing?"

"Good lord, are you out of your mind? Bringing me a dead magpie first thing in the morning? . . ." The woman keeps shaking her head. The dog, curled up on the cushion beneath the sewing machine, gets up and starts yapping at the visitor.

Back in the alley she continues to hold the bird, sensing it's still breathing. She can't bring herself to dump it.

Suddenly she stops where the sun is shining down diagonally and lifts her gathered hands toward the sky.

The feathers glisten in the sunlight, reminding her of sparkles in the ashes of the pea coals in Manchuria.

The girls' blood and the pea coals were what glistened in the comfort station.

❋

For nine days now she's been leaving right after lunch, anticipating an encounter with the girl as she roams the alleys of 15-*bŏnji*. But the girl just doesn't show up. Lately she's having dreams where she wanders the alleys in search of her. She guesses the girl might have moved but also wonders if something has happened to her.

She has no clue why she fixates on this nameless girl—after all she's long since lost all sense of attachment or kinship to anyone.[2] Her affection for her sisters is gone as well. Unable to breathe a word to them about her past made her ill at ease and distant from the nephews she saw a few times a year. She became an outlier and found it difficult even to make a friend.

She sometimes waits for the girl in the alley where she was gifted with the paper-pulp mask. She tries squatting against the wall where she found the girl squatting that time. She once waited more than two hours but the girl didn't appear.

Steeped in disappointment at not seeing the girl, she trudges down an alley and finds a pile of trash. Discards by a family that moved out? There's broken furniture, an electric rice cooker, a fry pan, dishes, a badminton racket, a stack of children's books, and more.

And a baby! She hurries over only to find it's a rubber doll. The doll's face is awash with a lovely smile for all the world to see, as if unaware it's been abandoned. She puts it to her bosom and pets it.

"Poor baby, where's your mommy and daddy?"[3]

No answer.

"How would you like to live with me?"[4] she whispers.

And then she looks up to see the girl standing in front of her. The girl is in her small yellow dress, and she's gazing not at her but at the doll. Now that she's finally encountered the girl, she feels pressured to escape from her.

"Are you on your way home from school?"

The girl doesn't respond.

She wants to lavish the girl with an amiable smile, but her hardened facial muscles can't rise to the task.

"Where do you live?"

No response.

"How old are you?"

"I'm 12."

And soon to be 13. This makes her uneasy.

"*Halmoni*, how old are you?"

"Me?"

The girl nods.

"13," she murmurs without realizing what she's saying.

"What? 13?" The girl's cheeks puff up and release a burst of laughter. Setting the doll down, she hurries off in a fluster.

Feeling guilty about abandoning the doll, she returns to the alley but finds neither doll nor girl.

13

SHE'S LYING ALL alone on the floor.
She's been lying there so long she can't tell how long.

The girl with the short, dark bobbed hair has transported her back to the Manchurian comfort station, to the room that's more like a tent, the very place she's wanted so desperately to escape the last seventy years or more.

※

The soldiers were making a racket out in the hallway. Whenever the soldiers got too loud Pokcha ŏnni would pipe up. And now she was saying, "They must be from Osaka. Osaka guys sound just like Kyŏng-sang guys, it's so fucking annoying!"

The door rattled open and a slight, youthful soldier was shoved in. He looked embarrassed and scared. He pulled his pants down to the ankles, then back up to his knees. He searched her face as he rolled on a *sakku* and then he grabbed her by the hair and penetrated her as if he was hammering a post and thrust violently, once, twice, three times.

He clutched her hair more tightly and thrust a fourth time and then a fifth and his face turned scarlet like the tip of a match just ignited.

As soon as he was gone, another soldier came in. He reeked of *gaoliang*, and she imagined a liquor bottle with legs. Cackling, he pulled down his pants. "You have to use a *sakku*!" she quickly reminded him. He brought his face close and cursed her in Japanese. "I have a disease, so you need to use a *sakku*." She wanted to cry. He was too drunk to stand up straight, and to keep his balance he sank his glistening metal teeth into her shoulder.

The third soldier stank not of *gaoliang* but of body odor. And a foul smell issued from between his teeth. When she turned her head aside, he forced it back toward him and glued his frenzied eyes to hers. At the height of his ecstasy he finally closed his eyes, erasing her.

The door rattled, wobbling like a tooth decayed to the root.

The fourth soldier had a mustache. "You smell like a frog," he muttered as he entered her. To her he smelled like a cat. The cat climbed onto the frog.

The fifth soldier called out a series of names, all of them female—Toyoko, Eiko, Miyako, Hanako. . . . His sisters, she assumed.

"Chieko!" he cried out.

"Who's she?" she asked, her voice trembling with fright.

"My girlfriend when I was 20."

The sixth soldier flipped her on her back as if she was a dead frog. Burying his face in hers, he thrashed about as if he was swimming for his life. As he was leaving he kicked her in the side with his boot.

Soldier number seven shot as soon as he was inside her. He pulled up his pants reluctantly and with an indignant expression, as if he'd been short-changed, then stopped and had at her again. The door was flung open and slammed shut, as if it was about to be yanked from its hinges.

"Hey, hurry up, hurry! *Sassato, sassato!*"

"Why are you crying?" said the eighth soldier.

But the one in tears was not her but him.

"I hate it when girls cry. My mother did that every goddamn morning!"

The ninth soldier scratched his head and offered a polite greeting before entering her.

As the tenth soldier was about to penetrate her, he flinched as if from a branding iron. She couldn't tell if her body was hot to the touch or cold.

An officer in spectacles, his mustache looking like a tattoo, entered her and exclaimed, "You feel like a dead body! *Shinda onna mitaine!*"

When she moaned he growled, "Don't bother! *Doryokuwa suruna!*"

He put his hands around her neck and tightened his hold on her. "I always wanted to do it with a dead girl! *Shinda onnato shite mitakkata!*"

The tighter the officer's hands gripped her neck, the more purple the dead girl's face. He left after emptying his load of semen into the dead girl as if scattering old seed onto a cement-coated wasteland.

The officer was gone. The dead girl's belly swelled up and the dead girl dreamed about an animal, the way her mother used to when she got pregnant. The dead girl's mother said that when she was pregnant with her she had dreamed of a bunny white as snow hopping down the hill and jumping into her bosom.

"It was a bunny," the dead girl mumbled. But wasn't the tail too long for it to be a bunny?

"It was a cat." But weren't the hind legs too long for it to be a cat?

"It was a deer." But deer don't have three legs.

In an alley where no one lives anymore she sees a woman crying. She's never seen the woman before. The woman is holding a black plastic bag. She wonders what's inside. The woman looks about fifty. The ankles revealed beneath the woman's ivory-colored pants are knotted and swollen. Each strand of the woman's permed hair vibrates like a filament emitting thermal energy, and she feels charged by that energy.

Why would she be crying?

She feels she is inside the woman, crying herself as she lies inside the crying woman. Power lines stretch out above the woman's head; not one bird has come to rest on those lines. Whenever she sees a woman crying she feels she has known the woman from long before.

She waits until the woman leaves, then goes to stand where the woman was crying.

14

I T'S AROUND DINNERTIME when she nears the mini-mart and
sees a crowd gathered outside. Police cruisers have pulled up in
front. A lanky policeman and a man in a pullover are chatting. She
can see only their backs. A policeman with a stocky build is talking
on his cell phone. The man who runs the store sits in one of the chairs
outside the entrance. Women huddle nearby, their expressions grave.
Their clothing is casual, probably what they wear at home. The alteration shop woman is among them. Another woman points toward the
back of the store, perhaps to one of the houses lined up like a deck
of flower cards. A break-in? What could it be? She decides to hang
back behind a utility pole and watch. Suddenly the man in the pullover
turns and stares at her. She tries to conceal herself behind the pole. Just
as she feared, it's the man from the precinct office. Her heart jumps
and her legs feel weak.

Not until the police have left do the women scatter. And not until
the man from the precinct office finishes his soft drink and swaggers

down the alley does she emerge from behind the utility pole and approach the store.

"Did something happen?" she gingerly asks the mini-mart man, who is back to work, sweeping outside the store entrance.

"Did something happen?" The man parrots the question.

"Weren't those police cars? . . ."

"Oh yeah, the police. They discovered a bunch of Chinese illegals living in P'yŏnghwa Villa."

"Women?"

"Yeah, I've been wondering about them—women I've never seen before coming around late at night and buying *ramyŏn*. You should have seen the roundup . . . what a spectacle! You must have been sound asleep. The neighbors had themselves quite a show . . ."

"You said women were living there?"

"That's right."

"That's odd . . . I've never seen any signs of life there . . ."

She remembers strolling past P'yŏnghwa Villa a few days ago. It looked like nobody lived there.

"Did you need something?"

Unable to remember what she came for, she blurts, "Tofu . . . just one block."

"Again?"

"Excuse me?"

"That's what you bought yesterday. You need some meat, instead of tofu every day, that way you'll have more energy," he says as he hands her a black plastic bag with the tofu.

"How many women were there?"

"About twenty, I think they said. They strung 'em together like dried fish and hauled 'em off."

"What will happen to them?"

"They'll probably get sent back to where they came from."

"How were they discovered anyway?"

"You know, a guy from the city's been poking through all the houses doing a survey and trying to figure out who actually lives here, that's how."

The man goes inside to the room at the back of the store. She watches momentarily as he helps his wife up, then leaves.

All this time the women kept themselves out of sight—and she herself had no clue. She doesn't recall hearing, seeing, or smelling anything the times she's passed by P'yŏnghwa Villa. She looks up toward the building but can't see it; it's obscured by the other buildings.

She wonders if the women really are sent back to their home country. She's afraid it won't happen. Instead the women will slip into some other place where there's money to be made and return home when they're too old to be recognized by their husband and kids.

❊

She plods along and finds herself in the same alley where the woman was crying. Was that woman in the alley one of the P'yŏnghwa Villa occupants? She thinks so.

❊

She has a hunch she'll be next. As early as tonight, the police along with the man from the city will raid the house where she stays.

She turns on her cell phone and enters her nephew's number. He picks up immediately but says nothing.

"Hello, Nephew. . . . It's me."

Only then does he ask why she's calling. She tells him the man from the precinct office stopped by.

"What for, do you know?"

"You see," she mumbles before pausing—she can't recall the term *actual resident.*

"Why did he stop by?"

"To survey people . . . those who didn't report an address change . . ."

"Survey?"

"Yes, survey, people like you, there are quite a few people who registered their residence but don't actually live—"

"The man from the precinct office—I hope you didn't say anything to get him wondering?"

"Why would I do that?"

"If he comes back, just tell him you don't know anything."

She just listens.

"Just say flat out, 'I don't know anything.'"

"All right, sure."

It sounds like her nephew knows the 15-*bŏnji* redevelopment plan is history.

"How old are you, *Imo?*"

She doesn't answer.

"Can you tell me how old are you?"

"Ninety-three . . ."

"That old?"

It strikes her that he's shocked by the answer, but the next moment he's broaching the idea of a nursing home for her. When she doesn't respond to the unexpected suggestion, he hurriedly ends the call, saying he'll stop by before long.

A nursing home—that was probably her nephew's plan all along. And even if it wasn't, he'll do it anyway once he gets priority for a new apartment. She has no desire to go to a nursing home. She doesn't know how much longer she has to live and wants only to remain in the Western-style house living quietly till she dies.

☀

She learns that night on the nine o'clock news that the last one was hospitalized several days ago. Old age is finally taking its toll: the last one is bedridden and unable to take food. The camera captures her face as she lies on her side. The haggard face looks different from that of the woman who told people she loved flowers.

The last one's eyes are shut tight as though she's fast asleep, but suddenly they open and stare into space. The last one looks startled. Her mouth wiggles like that of a babbling baby, and she looks as though she has something she wishes ardently to say.

As far as she knows, ever since the last one went public she's been diligent about letting the world know what happened at the comfort station. And according to the newspaper, the last one even flew to a faraway land across the ocean and testified in a pretty *hanbok* about her experiences.

She wonders if the last one has a story she hasn't been able to tell until now. Or if perhaps she's just remembered something else to tell.

A few days ago she too had a sudden recollection, and it was enough to interfere with her sleep. The girls had been taken to the outpost, and three soldiers, cackling and jabbering, decided to have some fun with her as she emerged from the outhouse. She backpedaled when she saw them, and one of the men took a dagger from his waistband and mimicked slitting his throat. She drew near, faltering, and they dragged her into the woods, where the man with the knife continued to threaten her while a second soldier was cajoling her. The third one stopped them but took off his pants like the other two and was quick to do his business when his turn came.[1]

I want to see her. They say she no longer recognizes people but I think she'll recognize me. I think she'll know who I am and why I've come to see her.

Should she let the world know, before the last one departs, that there is another last one?

She has a mind to do so, to be a witness. But how? And why now? She's never said a word, hiding the truth this way, covering it up that way, she's grown helplessly old, and soon she herself will be at death's doorstep.[2]

She opens the drawer to the television stand and takes out a folded sheet of paper. As she unfolds it the words that are practically etched into the paper seem to jump out and compete for her attention.

I'm a victim too.

It took more than seventy years for her to write that down.

She wants to add something, but suddenly everything is blank.

If only she could, instead of words to tell she'd like her tilted uterus displayed.

Imagining someone sitting across from her, she begins to speak: "At first, when I was there,[3] in the beginning . . . how I was taken there—I don't tell anyone about Manchuria. I felt so ashamed[4] . . . I wasn't able to spill it out, even to my sisters. I don't want to go home, no one's there anymore. One of the girls reported that she was a comfort woman. That brought the TV people and the camera crews, and all the neighbors got to know about it. With her government assistance she had a house built. But a neighbor who used to visit her every day stopped coming. She learned the neighbor had called her a dirty cunt[5] and said she sold her pussy to have that house built."

She can no longer continue.

No words can express her torment.[6]

15

THE LAST ONE is out of her coma. For three weeks she recognized no one. She speaks in a labored, halting tone: "I can't allow myself to die—not with no one after me to speak . . ."[1]

The last one spends practically the whole day hooked up to oxygen. She herself feels pained but proud to see the last one without her oxygen mask, managing to utter one word and then the next, stitching the words together in an attempt to tell the world who she is. Standing next to the last one is a caretaker who observes her with concern.

"I am not a comfort woman."[2]

"I am Yun Kŭmshil."

The last one gasps for air, and the caretaker is quick to place the oxygen mask over her mouth. The caretaker lays the last one down as carefully as if she's handling an infant. Then she puts her mouth to the last one's ear, whispers something, removes the oxygen mask, and sits her up.

The last one stares straight ahead as if she's being photographed for a passport.

"I want to be happy until the very end."[3]

❈

As she sits in front of the mirror slowly combing her hair, she mumbles to herself, "Me too, I want to be happy."

It's the first time she's ever thought about wanting to live happily. The first time in her nearly century-long life.

Even if it's just a single day.

She reaches toward the mirror.

And passes her hand across the image of a face she feels belongs to someone else.

❈

As she's wiping the floor with a rag the television and the fluorescent light go out. She takes a candle and matches from the drawer of the television stand. She strikes a match, brings the flame to the wick, and the instant the candle lights she recalls the girl from the neighborhood.

The girl's face comes to mind lightning-like and just as quickly is gone, but she feels that in that brief instant she's said a prayer for her.

No need to bother with the circuit breaker. Instead, by the light of the candle she passes her fingers back and forth across the lower part of the mask, where the mouth should be.

She takes her nail clipper and brings its tiny file to the mask.

With the tip of the file she draws a line where the mouth should be. She traces the line, traces it again and again, and some fifty tries later an opening appears. *There.*

Relentlessly she widens the mouth, the tip of the nail file going back and forth, the opening growing almost imperceptibly. She stops when the hole is big enough for her tongue to go through.

She puts the mask over her face.

I want to be born a girl . . . once more, just once, I want to be born a girl.[4]

✻

She's been out on the veranda all day. Just in case the man from the city stops by. There's something she must tell him.

The banging on the gate awakens her. Her head jerks up and her eyes open toward the gate.

The yard and veranda are full of light and the mask resting in her lap has taken on a peculiar gleam. The mouth hole she cut out with the tip of the nail file flickers in the light.

A man's head is sticking up above the gate, but with the sun at his back his facial features are blurred. It has to be the man from the city, she tells herself—she had a hunch he would drop by. And he's the only one who comes by without advance notice except the meterman, and the meterman visited two days ago.

"Please open the gate."

She swallows heavily, then mechanically utters the words she's prepared: "You know . . . I live here . . ."

"What?!" There's a touch of irritation to the voice.

"This . . . is where I live . . ."

"I can't hear you!"

"This is where I . . . I . . . live . . ."

"I said I can't hear you!"

She's in no mood to open the gate. She doesn't want to let the man from the city inside.

"Please open the gate!"

Stubbornly she holds her position, as if fixed by a spike to the veranda's wooden floor.

The man shakes the gate in exasperation.

She tries to restrain her racing heart, and when she's regained her composure, she says yet again, "This is where I live."

"*Imo!* It's me!"

What? It's not the man from the city?

"Open up."

She isn't inclined to let her nephew in either, but she can't just sit there. She gets up, but in the process the mask falls to the floor.

Instead of moving toward the gate, she plops herself back down on the veranda. Clutching her skirt with both hands, she tries to make herself as small as possible.

"*Imo!* Come *on, Imo!*"

She imagines the rattling of the gate echoing throughout the neighborhood.

No one can force her out from this house, she tells herself. Not the city guy, not her nephew from P'yŏngt'aek, not the owner she's never seen.

She forever longs to return home. Even in this home she longs to return home. She panics at the prospect of never returning home.[5]

The ancestral home she wanted to return to at least in spirit was still there, but not for her.

Not long ago this Western-style house—in which she has never officially resided—began to feel like the home to which she so longed to return.

She doesn't want to be sent out of a home to which she returned after well over seventy years.

Seeing that she's unwilling to open the gate, her nephew climbs over the wall. He strides toward where she's planted herself on the veranda.

His hiking boots tromping on the mask, he grabs her shoulders and shakes her.

"*Imo!*"

The mask with the mouth she labored to create last night lies mercilessly crushed beneath his foot.

✳

As she gazes vacantly at the seeds she collected last fall from a vacant home, she's struck by the realization that she is not alone but instead is surrounded by all of creation—the sky, the earth, the air, light, wind, water, seeds, and so much more.

And yet she *feels* even more alone.

All alone.

Once on television she saw images of the earth as seen from outer space. She knows the earth is round, but round like what? A baby pumpkin? An egg? An apple? A bead? And she wondered what color she could call it. The images she saw on television were not a single color but an indistinct blend of white, blue, orange, and green.

She held her breath and watched and before she knew it her face was inches from the screen as she wondered where all the houses were, and the people, and the birds on a wing.

It occurs to her that the earth is like a seed. And inside this seed called Earth there is water, there is land, and there are trees. Birds are flying, rabbits are nibbling grass, moles are tunneling, horses are jumping, and ants are marching.

To her the inside of the seed called Earth is beautiful and yet ugly.

Is it the same inside a cockscomb seed, beautiful and yet ugly?

She mutters to the seed, "Look here, there's one more who's left . . ."

Like the astronauts viewing the earth from outer space, she wants to see herself from the outside. Just as the earth looks utterly different from space, she wonders if she would look different if she saw herself from the outside.

⁂

Strolling in the alley, she flinches. Something reddish is wrapped around the metal handle of a gate. Her first thought is that it looks like a scorched hand hanging from the handle. She feels her hair standing on end as she inches closer. It's a mesh bag. But there's no kitten inside. The mesh bags she comes across in the alleys invariably contain a kitten.

She walks up to the gate and puts her face so close to the bag she feels like the bag is forming a noose around her neck. She wonders if there actually is a kitten in the bag and her eyesight is so bad she can't see it.

But if someone set it free, then who could it be?
Who?

16

GOING THROUGH THE neatly folded clothing in her wardrobe, she selects a brown pleated skirt and a pink knit cardigan and lays them out on the floor. From the basket heaped with socks she picks out a pair of white ones. The pink cardigan is her favorite, perfect for spring and fall.

As she fits the egg-flower buttons into the holes, her hands stiffen. Only now does she remember the exact number of men who came and went from her that first day, when she was 13 years old and had yet to experience her first menstrual flow.

Seven in all.[1] She bled more that day than she did later when her menstrual flow started.[2]

Number seven was an officer, a man who looked older than her father.

She steps down from the veranda to the yard holding a box inside a wrapping cloth the color of apricots. In the box is the set of long underwear she has kept all this time for the Chinese widower.

She hesitates at the gate, remembering her nephew is supposed to stop by today.

He visited two days ago and told her in no uncertain terms she was not to go anywhere today; instead the two of them were going somewhere.

"Where to?"

"To a nice place."

"A nice place?" she asked, recalling what Aesun had said on the train to Manchuria. Aesun had assumed she was going to "a nice place," a factory where she could earn money.

"You get your meals there and they give you a bath and a nurse gives you medication and shots if you're not feeling well."

She didn't respond.

"You'll make a lot of friends there, so you won't be lonely and bored. Three square meals, you can rest easy, and that's it."

She shook her head, her expression telling him no, but he ignored her.

"They provide everything. All you need to pack is your valuables and a change of clothing."

No matter how good the place mentioned by her nephew, she doesn't want to go there.

At the "nice place" Aesun had anticipated, her body became a graffiti board. With needle and ink the Japanese soldiers inscribed her belly, vulva, and tongue with tattoos.[3]

At that place the girls' bodies were not their own.[4]

She feels resentful toward her nephew but wishes she didn't. She doesn't want to resent or feel hate toward anyone in this world.[5]

But she cannot forgive what happened to her.[6]

If I heard those words, could I forgive?

Those words had to come from a certain source and no other, not even God in Heaven.

❀

Keeping to a sun-lit alley, she places her hand against the wall and breathes deeply. The leaning, crumbling wall has become a momentary support. Her energy level isn't what it used to be.

The old man is nowhere to be seen. But his yard is if anything even more littered with heaps of wire, and with the cloth and copper he's stripped from it, than it was a month ago. Her gaze lands at a plastic bowl filled with rusty nails—more loot from the empty houses.

She leaves the box with the long underwear next to the bowl. When it gets cold he instead of the Chinese widower will wear it.

A half-collapsed home comes into sight down the alley. She's not sure if it's collapsing on its own or undergoing demolition. Here and there in 15-*bŏnji* she sees such houses. And there are places where the demolition is complete except for the wall fronting the alley, standing fortress-like.

The brick walls of this house and the wall facing the alley are mostly gone and only the skeleton of a room remains. There's no ceiling, and all that's left of the windows is shattered glass. A precarious door frame is the only indication that the space used to be a room.

She'll need to hurry if she's to return by lunchtime, but her feet are not in rushing mode.

The room she sees looks like a uterus.

She imagines her own uterus dropped into that room. Her feet just aren't moving; instead she hears the rattling of a gate. It sounds like the gate of her house.

✵

The minibus that runs between 15-*bŏnji* and the subway station leaves every twenty minutes. The 15-*bŏnji* residents generally take this bus to the subway station if they're going somewhere. Waiting with her for the bus is a boy who looks like a high school kid. Wearing earbuds and seemingly disinterested in the sounds drifting about the world outside, he glares at the toes of his shoes. From a few steps away she can sense his erupting dissatisfaction and rebellious heart.

He must have been almost the same age as that student. Only once did a Korean soldier come and go from her at the comfort station in Manchuria; he was from Chaech'ŏn, North Ch'ungch'ŏng Province. The Japanese 志, written in red inside a circle on his armband, meant he was a so-called student volunteer taken into the Japanese army,[7] according to Kŭmbok *ŏnni*. There was a Korean soldier who came once in a long while to Kŭmbok *ŏnni*, and she referred to him as *oppa*, as if he were her older brother. Kŭmbok *ŏnni* said that she and *oppa* would have a smoke and talk about home and end up crying. When the soldier from Chaech'ŏn entered her she put her hand to his chest and her fingers felt all too fully the cracking and breaking of his heart. She thought she would see him a couple more times, but she never saw him again. And then Kŭmbok *ŏnni's oppa* stopped coming. The girls believed that if a familiar face no longer showed up, then its owner must have died in battle.[8]

The bus stop is located where three alleys come together. She looks about and spots a magpie nest resting precariously among the branches of a gingko tree. With its sooty color and circular shape it resembles a broken-down bamboo basket, and it looks for all the world like it's been abandoned. Perhaps it was built by one of the magpies Nabi brought her from its hunting expeditions. And when her thoughts reach this far, a question occurs to her:

Whoever taught these birds to fly around gathering twigs and then weave them into a nest?

This "in the beginning" question is followed by a train of similar questions:

Whoever taught newborn puppies to nurse even before they open their eyes? Whoever taught ladybugs to lay their eggs on leaves? Whoever taught brood hens to sit atop their eggs?

The bus trundles up the slope, makes a great half circle, then lurches to a stop in front of her.

As she absently watches passengers getting off, she feels a gentle tap on the shoulder.

"Where're you heading, ma'am?" It's the woman from the alteration shop, just back from market, to judge from several black plastic bags she's holding. From one of them comes the smell of fish.

"I'm going to see someone . . ."

"Who might that be?" The woman looks at her dubiously—because of the magpie incident?

"Someone—"

"Yes, but who?"

"Someone I have to see . . ."

The woman cocks her head, doubtful, and with downcast eyes examines the brown pleated skirt and the pink knit cardigan. "I don't know who the lucky one is, but you sure are lovely, all dolled up like a newlywed."

"A newlywed? Me? . . ."

"You're not going very far, are you?"

"Far?"

"Yes, far."

"No, I'm not going far . . ." Poker-faced, she shakes her head.

"Please be careful. Remember the number of the bus, and if you get lost, be sure to ask someone." It's as if the woman is drilling a child.

"Of course."

"Aren't you getting on?"

She boards the bus, feeling as if the woman's words are ushering her on. There are vacant seats in front but she goes all the way to the rear to sit.

The bus glides down the road it just labored up. Sunshine fills the interior. Her eyelashes flicker in the blinding light and a name flutters like a butterfly onto her tongue.

P'unggil . . .

Her name in the ancestral village before she was taken to Manchuria at the age of 13. She always thought it was part of her when she emerged from her mother's womb, as much a part of her as her arms and legs, absolutely inseparable. In her village she thought she could hear even the goats and the sparrows calling her P'unggil.

P'unggil-a!

Her memory of Kŭmbok ŏnni calling her name is so vivid she looks around the interior of the bus to see if Kŭmbok ŏnni is there.

Even after Pongae was swept away in the river, *haha* and *otosan* continued to have the girls taken "on business" to the outpost. It hadn't rained for some time and the river was down but still turbid.

They were about to pass a riverside village. The village was draped in an eerie silence, and the girls wondered if anyone lived there—until they saw a lone woman facing the river. The woman's black hair fell to her waist, and all she herself could think of was Pongae.

"It's Pongae," she murmured.

Hearing this, Hyangsuk lifted her head from where she'd buried it against her upraised knees. Hyangsuk hadn't seen Pongae disappear into the river. Hyangsuk picked her ear with a finger, then buried her head in her lap again.

"I want to go home. I miss Mom's cooking. I want my scoop of barley rice with the kimchi on top,"[9] whimpered Kunja.

She herself wanted to wave to the woman, wanted to wave before the woman grew distant. And so she rose, and the moment she raised her hand she fell into the water. Whether she stumbled or whether a gust of wind was responsible, she never knew.

The current was like a noose around her neck and she pushed at the water, at the same time reaching with her feet for the river bottom but feeling only a fathomless emptiness. Seaweed-like vegetation wrapped itself about her ankles and she was pulled under. She couldn't see her nose in front of her face, the water was so murky, and then suddenly it turned clear, revealing a bier adorned with flowers. Inside lay a girl, she herself. Her flower-bedecked face was chubby like that of a baby who has feasted on mommy's milk and dozed off.

So this is how it ends.[10] At the very instant she accepted her death she heard a voice blast out.

"I got her!"

Hands pulled at clumps of her hair.

"P'unggil-a! P'unggil-a! . . ."

"Open your eyes, come on."

Sprawled out on the ferry deck, she registered the girls' faces.

"You're alive!"

"P'unggil *ŏnni*'s alive!" Yŏngsun bawled.

"Do you know who we are?" said Kŭmbok *ŏnni*.

She felt Kŭmbok *ŏnni* slapping her and that's when she realized she was alive. Looking up at the sky, she began to sob.

"Don't cry." Kŭmbok ŏnni sat her up and pulled her close. Rubbing her back, Kŭmbok ŏnni said, "You're not dead, you're still here, so there's no need to cry."[11]

Just do what haha *says.* Only now, more than seventy years later, does she feel she understands Kŭmbok ŏnni's entreaty: *You have to survive, no matter what.*

It occurs to her that in going to see the last one she's going to see Kŭmbok ŏnni—and Haegŭm, and Tongsuk ŏnni, and Hanok ŏnni, and Hunam ŏnni, and Kisuk ŏnni . . .

What should I say first? That I really missed you? That I was in Manchuria too? . . .

She's finally on her way. It's like this journey has been in the back of her mind her whole life. It's thanks to the woman at the Seoul Beauty Parlor that she learned how to get to the hospital where the last one was admitted. Coincidentally, it's the university hospital where the woman goes for her regular check-up. She herself assumed the last one lived in another city. And that that's where the hospital is. Why didn't it occur to her that the last one might be living nearby?

Though she so longs to meet her, the prospect of actually doing so has her trembling with fear.

❈

The minibus stops in front of a drugstore and half a dozen passengers scramble on. The empty seats are filling but the one next to her remains unoccupied. And then a woman as petite and fetching as Haegŭm follows a boy on board. She herself taps the seat next to her to indicate it's vacant. The other woman, who's been looking for an empty seat, approaches and sits her boy there. The boy glances at she herself with gentle mischief in his eyes and she responds with a beaming smile.

She feels languid and the dream she awakened from at daybreak comes back to her. Holding the hand of the girl in 15-*bŏnji*, she walks toward a river. At the riverside she sits the girl down, then sits beside her. Cupping water from the river in her hands, she washes the girl's face. Dark, scummy water drips from it. She keeps washing the girl's face until the water dripping from it is clear.

Before she knows it the minibus has entered a busy intersection. Looking out at the world beyond the window, she realizes anew:

That she still lives in fear.[12]

And she's still at the comfort station in Manchuria, a 13-year-old girl.[13]

AFTERWORD

Bruce and Ju-Chan Fulton

Why did it take seventy-five years for a Korean novel to be written about the Korean girls who endured sexual slavery during the Pacific War? This was the first question addressed to us in an interview by Justin Maki, New York City correspondent for the Kyodo News Agency, in late 2018. The same question could likely be asked about other traumas endured by Koreans in their modern history: the subject matter is simply too painful to write about.

If an experience is too painful to write about, imagine how much more painful it could be to make that experience public. Compound one individual's experience with the experiences of the millions of individuals directly affected by one or more of the man-made catastrophes afflicting the occupants of the Korean Peninsula in the modern era—the recruitment of young men and women into sexual servitude, forced labor, and military service by Imperial Japan from the late 1930s through 1945; the massacre of civilians in both Koreas before and during the Korean War (1950–53); the massacre of citizens of the city of Kwangju, South Chŏlla Province, by elite South Korean military forces in May 1980; the torture apparatus and extrajudicial executions used in South Korea from its birth in 1948 until the democratization of the political process there in the late 1980s—and we have a persuasive answer to the rhetorical question posed by historian Bruce Cumings in his foreword to our 2009 volume of trauma fiction in contemporary Korea, *The Red Room*: "Is it possible for an entire nation to have post-traumatic stress disorder?"

From a distance it is all too easy to consign awareness of historical outrages to a dim corner of our consciousness. Not until we are confronted with direct evidence of a disaster—the written or oral reports of the survivors, victims' names on tombstones, works of art and literature offering us images and words of the victims, all of which we might understand as testimony—are we forced to acknowledge the magnitude of the trauma and the urgency of the need for healing.

Our first encounter with testimony by a Korean survivor of sexual servitude during the Pacific War was occasioned by a 1995 essay, "To Live without Shame" by Hwang Kŭmju, which appeared in the short-lived but influential journal *Muae*. But not until we discovered the myriad voices whose testimony constitutes much of the detail in Kim Soom's 2016 novel *Han myŏng* did we begin to appreciate the courage of those among them, starting with Kim Haksun in 1991, to go public with their testimony. And only then, at the realization that only thirty-one of the self-reported survivors of sexual servitude were still alive, did we realize how urgent it was to bring this novel to an English-language readership.

We soon found, though, that our sense of urgency was not shared by publishers (and we ultimately approached thirty-two of them)—in spite of their knowledge that *One Left*, our translation of *Han myŏng*, had been awarded a 2018 PEN/Heim Translation Fund grant—only the second Korean project to be thus recognized since the endowment of this fund in 2003. "How are we to market this book?" they asked. As a historical study or as a work of literature? One publisher (which now accounts for more literature in translation than any other American publisher) found it more of a history book and, citing unnamed "stakeholders," suggested we find an academic publisher. We thought this an excellent suggestion, for we had published several volumes of Korean fiction in translation through the same academic press that had published an English translation of Yoshimi Yoshiaki's pathbreaking work (mentioned by Bonnie Oh in the foreword to this volume) on sexual slavery in the Japanese military during World War II. This publisher, though, perhaps influenced by the assertion of an outside reader of the translation that the novel was voyeuristic, remarked that the "comfort women" issue had been sensationalized in both Korea and the United States. The publisher was concerned that readers of *One Left* would consider it conventional and unnuanced. We were therefore advised to seek a non-academic publisher.

Far from being an unnuanced treatment of the "comfort women," Kim Soom's novel deserves credit for the narrative distance maintained between author and subject matter through the use of the survivors' voices. Indeed it was Kim's decision to structure her narrative on the foundation of the voices of the survivors themselves that distinguishes her novel from the few English-language novels in which we find images of the survivors. The novel is also objective in giving voice, albeit sparingly, to the Japanese soldiers, who in many cases were also coerced into service on behalf of Imperial Japan's war effort. Moreover, those who fear that the novel is a case of Japan bashing should note that among the various characters responsible for coercing the Korean girls into sexual servitude, either through blandishments involving a "good job" in a factory or through threats, are Koreans themselves—a fact demonstrated through research conducted by Chunghee Sarah Soh for her pioneering study *The Comfort Women*.

In recent years it has become increasingly common to find the word *necessary* embedded in back-cover blurb-speak for works of fiction and nonfiction alike. This overused term is appropriate for *One Left*, though, for two reasons. First, against all odds, the process of truth and reconciliation is gaining momentum in South Korea, and literature remains a viable channel through which truth can be illuminated and the first steps toward healing from trauma, both individual and collective, can be taken. Second, it is necessary for an American audience to realize that Korean history, society, and culture, no less than those of any other nation, maintain a tradition of co-optation of the female body for the "greater good" of the dynasty or nation. To this day the United States continues to play a role in this co-optation in the form of militarized prostitution, by virtue of the American military presence on Korean soil since Liberation in 1945.

One Left is our translation of the Korean title, literally "one person," of Kim Soom's novel. "One left" reverberates in a variety of ways: At the end of the novel, among the registered survivors of sexual servitude only one is left, and she lies on her deathbed. The protagonist wishes to assure this "last one" that after her passing there will still be at least "one left," she herself. "One left" also refers to each of the hundreds of thousands of Korean girls who left the ancestral village and the Korean Peninsula for truncated lives behind military lines. The final scene in the novel also involves a departure: the narrator leaves for the hospital in which the "last one" lies, there to testify to her that she herself is left. This departure, though, involves a fundamental reclamation of agency, in that the protagonist recovers her own given name, P'unggil, a name by which she has not been addressed for some seventy years. In this way, author Kim Soom has launched a process of recovery that will return to historical memory not only the hundreds of thousands of individuals who experienced sexual servitude in the Pacific War but more generally the millions of individuals, male as well as female, in Korea and throughout the world who have been traumatized by ideological dogma and state violence.

The euphemism *comfort women* has long been used in reference to those who experienced sexual servitude during the Pacific War. These individuals might more accurately be thought of as girls, at least at the time they entered servitude. It should be pointed out that the ages mentioned in the text are to be understood in terms of calendar years—that is, the number of years in which an individual has lived at least one day. One may then assume, for example, that a girl identified as 14 in the text would by the Western counting of age be 13.

A number of individuals deserve credit for helping this translation of Kim Soom's novel see the light of day. We are grateful to the selection committee of the 2018 PEN/Heim Translation Fund grants and to Justin Maki of Kyodo News Agency, who first became aware of our translation through news of this grant. Mr. H. Lee, a Korean official in Seattle, spent long hours elucidating the arcane particulars of Korean versus American tax law. Author Kim Soom handled endless pages of queries with aplomb, and her agent, Rosa Han, mediated negotiations among four parties—author, translators, Korean publisher, and American publisher—a thankless task at a time when the publication of Korean literature in English translation has become an increasingly mercenary enterprise. Eiko Cope assisted with the occasional Japanese phrase in the Korean text. Chunghee Sarah Soh, professor of anthropology at San Francisco State University, and Bonnie Oh, emerita distinguished professor of Korean studies at the Edmund A. Walsh School of Foreign Service, Georgetown University, encouraged us from the outset. A residency at Seoul Art Space, Yeonhui, in May 2019 and a residency at the T'oji Cultural Center, outside the city of Wŏnju, Korea, from September to October 2019 provided us with the opportunity to polish the translation. Bruce Fulton wishes to acknowledge the extensive background research conducted by Ju-Chan Fulton. Finally, Larin McLaughlin, editor in chief of the University of Washington Press, is to be commended for wholeheartedly taking on a project on ground that dozens of other publishers, commercial and academic, feared to tread.

REFERENCES

Cumings, Bruce. Foreword to *The Red Room: Stories of Trauma in Contemporary Korea*, translated by Bruce and Ju-Chan Fulton, vii–xii. Honolulu: University of Hawai'i Press, 2009.

Hwang Kŭmju. "To Live without Shame." Translated by Heinz Insu Fenkl from a Korean version edited by Chung Chin-sung. *Muae: A Journal of Transcultural Production* 1 (1995): 194–203. Hwang's testimonial is accompanied by an essay by Chung Chin-sung, "An Overview of the Colonial and Socio-economic Background of Japanese Military Sex Slavery in Korea" (pp. 204–15) and a portfolio of paintings by Miran Kim (pp. 216–20).

Soh, Chunghee Sarah. *The Comfort Women: Sexual Violence and Postcolonial Memory in Korea and Japan.* Chicago: University of Chicago Press, 2008.

NOTES

PROLOGUE

1 Ri Sangok: Ito Takashi, "Sŭlp'ŭn kwihyang: Pungnyŏk halmŏni ŭi chŭngŏn" [Sad return home: Testimony by elderly North Korean women], part 1, *Nyusŭ t'ap'a mokkyŏkcha tŭl*, March 4, 2016.

2 Kxx (pseudonym; b. 1923): *Tŭllinayo? Yŏldu sonyŏ ŭi iyagi: Ilbon'gun wianbu p'ihae kusul kirokchip* [Can you hear us? The stories of twelve girls: An oral history of comfort-woman victims of the Japanese military] (Seoul: Taeil hangjaenggi kangje tong'wŏn p'ihae chosa mit kugoe kangje tong'wŏn hisaengja tŭng chiwŏn wiwŏnhoe, 2013).

CHAPTER 1

1 Pak Turi: *Kangje ro kkŭllyŏgan Chosŏnin kun wianbu tŭl* [Forcibly recruited Korean military comfort women], vol. 2, comp. Hanguk chŏngshindae munje taech'aek hyŏbŭihoe and Hanguk chŏngshindae yŏn'guhoe (P'aju: Han'ul, 1997).

2 Chin Kyŏngp'aeng: *Kangje ro kkŭllyŏgan Chosŏnin kun wianbu tŭl*, vol. 2; Kang Muja: *Kangje ro kkŭllyŏgan Chosŏnin kun wianbu tŭl*, vol. 2.

3 Chin Kyŏngp'aeng: *Kangje ro kkŭllyŏgan Chosŏnin kun wianbu tŭl*, vol. 2; Kang Muja: *Kangje ro kkŭllyŏgan Chosŏnin kun wianbu tŭl*, vol. 2.

4 Ch'oe Kapsun: *Kangje ro kkŭllyŏgan Chosŏnin kun wianbu tŭl*, vol. 4, *Kiŏk ŭro tashi ssŭnŭn yŏksa*, comp. Hanguk chŏngshindae munje taech'aek hyŏbŭihoe 2000nyŏn Ilbon'gun sŏngno e chŏnbŏm yŏsŏng kukche pŏpchŏng Hanguk wiwŏnhoe chŭngŏn t'im (Seoul: P'ulpit, 2000).

5 Kang Muja: *Kangje ro kkŭllyŏgan Chosŏnin kun wianbu tŭl*, vol. 2.

6 Kim Yŏngsuk: "Sŭlp'ŭn kwihyang," part 1.

7 Kim Poktong: *Kangje ro kkŭllyŏgan Chosŏnin kun wianbu tŭl*, vol. 2.

8 Ri Kyŏngsaeng: "Sŭlp'ŭn kwihyang," part 1.

9 Hwang Sŏnsun: "Nunmul lo saeng ŭl ponaenŭn wianbu halmŏni" [An elderly comfort woman living a tearful life], EBS News broadcast, October 7, 2013.

10 Dxx (pseudonym): *Tŭllinayo?*

11 Yi Oksŏn (b. 1925): *Ch'ungch'ŏng int'ŏnet shinmun hamkke hanŭn Ch'ungbuk*, August 4, 2015.

12 Yi Oksŏn (b. 1927): *Yŏksa rŭl mandŭnŭn iyagi: Ilbon'gun "wianbu" yŏsŏng tŭl ŭi kyŏnghŏm kwa kiŏk* [History-making stories: Experiences and memories of the "comfort women" of the Japanese military], vol. 6 of *Ilbon'gun "wianbu" chŭngŏnjip* [Testimony of the "comfort women" of the Japanese military] (Seoul: Yŏsŏng kwa inkwŏn, 2004).

13 Kang Muja: *Kangje ro kkŭllyŏgan Chosŏnin kun wianbu tŭl*, vol. 2.

14 Ch'oe Myŏngsun: *Kangje ro kkŭllyŏgan Chosŏnin kun wianbu tŭl*, vol. 1, comp. Hanguk chŏngshindae munje taech'aek hyŏbŭihoe and Hanguk chŏngshindae yŏn'guhoe (Seoul: Han'ul, 1993).

15 Brand of leaf tobacco sold by the Monopoly Bureau of the Japanese Government-General in Seoul.

16 Kim Üllye: *Kangje ro kkŭllyŏgan Chosŏnin kun wianbu tŭl* [Forcibly recruited Korean military comfort women], vol. 3, comp. Hanguk chŏngshindae munje taech'aek hyŏbŭihoe and Hanguk chŏngshindae yŏn'guhoe (P'aju: Han'ul, 1999).

17 Kim Sunak: Kim Sŏnnim, *Ilbon'gun "wianbu" Kim Sunak: Nae sok ŭn amu to morŭndak'ai* [Kim Sunak, a comfort woman for the Japanese military: No one knows my heart]. Chŏngshindae halmŏni wa hamkke hanŭn shimin moim, 2008.

18 Ixx (pseudonym): *Tŭllinayo?*

19 Mun Okchu: *Kangje ro kkŭllyŏgan Chosŏnin kun wianbu tŭl*, vol. 1.

CHAPTER 2

1 Yi Oksŏn (b. 1925): CNN interview, December 12, 2015.

2 Bxx (pseudonym; b. 1927): *Tŭllinayo?*

3 Kxx (pseudonym; b. 1923): *Tŭllinayo?*

4 Yi Yongsu: "Toraji kkot iyagi" [Story of a bellflower], testimony.

5 Hwang Kŭmju: *Kangje ro kkŭllyŏgan Chosŏnin kun wianbu tŭl*, vol. 1.

6 Bxx (pseudonym; b. 1929): *Tŭllinayo?*

7 Bxx (pseudonym; b. 1927): *Tŭllinayo?*

8 Axx (pseudonym; b. 1930): *Tŭllinayo?*

9 Kim Ünjin: *Kangje ro kkŭllyŏgan Chosŏnin kun wianbu tŭl*, vol. 2.

10 Jxx (pseudonym): *Tŭllinayo?*; Bxx (pseudonym; b. 1924): *Tŭllinayo?*

11 Axx (pseudonym; b. 1930): *Tŭllinayo?*

12 Hwang Kŭmju: *Kangje ro kkŭllyŏgan Chosŏnin kun wianbu tŭl,* vol. 1.

13 Bxx (pseudonym; b. 1927): *Tŭllinayo?*

14 Bxx (pseudonym; b. 1930): *Tŭllinayo?*

15 Yi Kijŏng: article in the *Chungang ilbo,* September 9, 2015.

16 Kim Sunak: *Yŏksa rŭl mandŭnŭn iyagi.*

17 Pxx (pseudonym): *Tŭllinayo?*

18 Hwang Kŭmju: *Kangje ro kkŭllyŏgan Chosŏnin kun wianbu tŭl,* vol. 1.

19 Kim Pong'i: *Yŏksa rŭl mandŭnŭn iyagi.*

20 Kim Poktong: *Kangje ro kkŭllyŏgan Chosŏnin kun wianbu tŭl,* vol. 2.

21 Kang Muja: *Kangje ro kkŭllyŏgan Chosŏnin kun wianbu tŭl,* vol. 2.

22 Kim Hwaja: *Yŏksa rŭl mandŭnŭn iyagi.*

23 Kim Hwaja: *Yŏksa rŭl mandŭnŭn iyagi.*

24 Im Chŏngja: *Yŏksa rŭl mandŭnŭn iyagi.*

25 Yi Oksŏn (b. 1927): *Yŏksa rŭl mandŭnŭn iyagi.*

26 Ha Sunnyŏ: *Kangje ro kkŭllyŏgan Chosŏnin kun wianbu tŭl,* vol. 1.

27 Kim Yŏngsuk: "Sŭlp'ŭn kwihyang," part 1.

28 Kim Hwaja: *Yŏksa rŭl mandŭnŭn iyagi.*

29 Kim Hwaja: *Yŏksa rŭl mandŭnŭn iyagi.*

30 Yi Tŭngnam: *Kangje ro kkŭllyŏgan Chosŏnin kun wianbu tŭl,* vol. 1.

31 Kim Hwaja: *Yŏksa rŭl mandŭnŭn iyagi.*

32 Kim Yŏngsuk: "Pukch'ŭk chonggun wianbu p'ihaeja Kim Yŏngsuk halmŏni chŭngŏn" [Testimony of the elderly Kim Yŏngsuk, a North Korean comfort woman and victim of the Japanese military], *Minjok* 21 (March 2002).

33 Axx (pseudonym; b. 1930): *Tŭllinayo?*

34 Yi Yongnyŏ: *Kangje ro kkŭllyŏgan Chosŏnin kun wianbu tŭl,* vol. 1.

35 Yi Yŏngsuk: *Kangje ro kkŭllyŏgan Chosŏnin kun wianbu tŭl,* vol. 3.

36 Kim Sunak: *Nae sok ŭn amu to morŭndak'ai.*

37 Kim Sunak: *Nae sok ŭn amu to morŭndak'ai.*

38 Axx (pseudonym; b. 1925): *Tŭllinayo?*

39 Cho Yunok: *Kagoship'ŭn kohyang ŭl nae pal lo kŏrŏ mot kago* [My feet could not take me home]. *Chŏngshindae halmŏni wa hamkke hanŭn shimin moim,* 2007.

40 Kim Poktong: *Kangje ro kkŭllyŏgan Chosŏnin kun wianbu tŭl,* vol. 2.

41 Kim Poktong: *Kangje ro kkŭllyŏgan Chosŏnin kun wianbu tŭl,* vol. 2.

42 Yi Sangok: *Kangje ro kkŭllyŏgan Chosŏnin kun wianbu tŭl,* vol. 1.

43 Kim Ch'unhŭi: *Kangje ro kkŭllyŏgan Chosŏnin kun wianbu tŭl,* vol. 2.

44 Cho Yunok: *Kagoship'ŭn kohyang.*

45 Hwang Kŭmju: *Ilje kangjŏmgi* [The Japanese occupation of Korea], comp. Pak To (Seoul: Nunpit, 2010).

46 Kwak Kŭmnyŏ: "Sŭlp'ŭn kwihyang," part 2, March 10, 2016.

47 Chŏng Oksŏn.

48 Kim Poktong: *Kangje ro kkŭllyŏgan Chosŏnin kun wianbu tŭl*, vol. 2.

CHAPTER 3

1 Yi Yongsu: *Kangje ro kkŭllyŏgan Chosŏnin kun wianbu tŭl*, vol. 1.

2 Yun Turi: *Kangje ro kkŭllyŏgan Chosŏnin kun wianbu tŭl*, vol. 1.

3 Bxx (pseudonym; b. 1927): *Tŭllinayo?*

4 Kim Ch'unhŭi: *Kangje ro kkŭllyŏgan Chosŏnin kun wianbu tŭl*, vol. 2.

5 Bxx (pseudonym; b. 1927): *Tŭllinayo?*

6 Yun Turi: *Kangje ro kkŭllyŏgan Chosŏnin kun wianbu tŭl*, vol. 1.

7 Hwang Kŭmju: *Ilje kangjŏmgi.*

8 Hwang Kŭmju: *Kangje ro kkŭllyŏgan Chosŏnin kun wianbu tŭl*, vol. 1; Yun Sunman: *Kiŏk ŭro tashi ssŭnŭn yŏksa.*

9 Hwang Kŭmju: *Kangje ro kkŭllyŏgan Chosŏnin kun wianbu tŭl*, vol. 1.

10 Kim Yŏngja: *Kiŏk ŭro tashi ssŭnŭn yŏksa.*

11 Kim Ŭnjin: *Kangje ro kkŭllyŏgan Chosŏnin kun wianbu tŭl*, vol. 2.

12 Mun Okchu: *Kangje ro kkŭllyŏgan Chosŏnin kun wianbu tŭl*, vol. 1.

13 Chang Chŏmdol: *Yŏksa rŭl mandŭnŭn iyagi.*

14 Kim Ch'unhŭi: *Kangje ro kkŭllyŏgan Chosŏnin kun wianbu tŭl*, vol. 2.

15 Yun Turi: *Kangje ro kkŭllyŏgan Chosŏnin kun wianbu tŭl*, vol. 1.

16 Chŏng Oksun: "Sŭlp'ŭn kwihyang," part 1.

17 Ch'oe Kapsun: *Kiŏk ŭro tashi ssŭnŭn yŏksa.*

18 Yun Sunman: *Kiŏk ŭro tashi ssŭnŭn yŏksa.*

19 Mun P'ilgi: *Kangje ro kkŭllyŏgan Chosŏnin kun wianbu tŭl*, vol. 1.

20 Yi Yŏngsuk: *Kangje ro kkŭllyŏgan Chosŏnin kun wianbu tŭl*, vol. 1.

21 Ch'oe Kapsun: *Kiŏk ŭro tashi ssŭnŭn yŏksa.*

22 Chŏng Oksun: Ito Takashi, "Chiok ŭi hyŏngbŏl poda tŏ ch'ittŏllinŭn Ilbon'gun ŭi manhaeng" [Japanese brutality, more horrifying than punishment in hell], *Hangyŏre* 21, October 22, 1998.

23 Ri Sangok: "Sŭlp'ŭn kwihyang," part 1.

24 Kim Ŭnjin: *Kangje ro kkŭllyŏgan Chosŏnin kun wianbu tŭl*, vol. 2.

25 Kim Ŭnjin: *Kangje ro kkŭllyŏgan Chosŏnin kun wianbu tŭl*, vol. 2.

26 Hxx (pseudonym): *Tŭllinayo?*

27 Bxx (pseudonym; b. 1929): *Tŭllinayo?*

28 Chin Kyŏngp'aeng: *Kangje ro kkŭllyŏgan Chosŏnin kun wianbu tŭl*, vol. 2.

29 Ri Kyŏngsaeng: "Sŭlp'ŭn kwihyang," part 1.

30 Ri Kyŏngsaeng: "Sŭlp'ŭn kwihyang," part 1.

31 Pak Yŏni: *Kangje ro kkŭllyŏgan Chosŏnin kun wianbu tŭl*, vol. 2.

32   Yi Yongnyŏ: *Kangje ro kkŭllyŏgan Chosŏnin kun wianbu tŭl*, vol. 1.

33   No Ch'ŏngja: *Yŏksa rŭl mandŭnŭn iyagi.*

34   Chin Kyŏngp'aeng: *Kangje ro kkŭllyŏgan Chosŏnin kun wianbu tŭl*, vol. 2.

35   Ch'oe Illye: *Kangje ro kkŭllyŏgan Chosŏnin kun wianbu tŭl*, vol. 2.

36   Kim Hwaja: *Yŏksa rŭl mandŭnŭn iyagi.*

37   Chen Tao (a Taiwanese comfort woman, victim of the Japanese military): "Kkŭnnajianŭn chŏnjaeng, Ilbon'gun wianbu" [Endless war, comfort women for the Japanese military], broadcast on *KBS p'anorama p'ŭllŏsŭ*, August 8, 2013.

38   Yŏ Pokshil: *Kangje ro kkŭllyŏgan Chosŏnin kun wianbu tŭl*, vol. 2.

39   Yi Sangok: *Kangje ro kkŭllyŏgan Chosŏnin kun wianbu tŭl*, vol. 1.

CHAPTER 4

1   Kxx (pseudonym; b. 1923): *Tŭllinayo?*

2   Pak Ch'asun: "Kohyang hŭngnaemsae matcha 'Arirang'. . . Hubaei sŏng 93se halmŏni" [The moment I smelled the earth of my native place I thought of the song "Arirang" . . . a 93-year-old former "comfort woman" in Hubai Province], *Chungang ilbo*, November 12, 2015.

3   Fxx (pseudonym): *Tŭllinayo?*

4   Fxx (pseudonym): *Tŭllinayo?*

5   Cho Yunok: *Kagoship'ŭn kohyang.*

6   Chang Chŏmdol: *Yŏksa rŭl mandŭnŭn iyagi.*

7   Yŏ Pokshil: *Kangje ro kkŭllyŏgan Chosŏnin kun wianbu tŭl*, vol. 2.

8   Axx (pseudonym; b. 1930): *Tŭllinayo?*

9   Cho Yunok: *Kagoship'ŭn kohyang.*

10   Kim Haksun.

11   Chang Chŏmdol: *Yŏksa rŭl mandŭnŭn iyagi.*

12   Ch'oe Myŏngsun: *Kangje ro kkŭllyŏgan Chosŏnin kun wianbu tŭl*, vol. 1.

13   Yun Turi: *Kangje ro kkŭllyŏgan Chosŏnin kun wianbu tŭl*, vol. 1.

14   Kim Poktong.

15   Chŏn Kŭmhwa: *Kangje ro kkŭllyŏgan Chosŏnin kun wianbu tŭl*, vol. 2.

16   Kim Poksŏn: *Kangje ro kkŭllyŏgan Chosŏnin kun wianbu tŭl*, vol. 1.

17   Yi Tŭngnam: *Kangje ro kkŭllyŏgan Chosŏnin kun wianbu tŭl*, vol. 1.

18   Chin Kyŏngp'aeng: *Kangje ro kkŭllyŏgan Chosŏnin kun wianbu tŭl*, vol. 2.

19   Ch'oe Illye: *Kangje ro kkŭllyŏgan Chosŏnin kun wianbu tŭl*, vol. 2; Pak Sŏun.

20   Kang Muja: *Kangje ro kkŭllyŏgan Chosŏnin kun wianbu tŭl*, vol. 2.

21   Zang Zhendu (a Chinese comfort woman and victim of the Japanese military): "Kkŭnnajianŭn chŏnjaeng, Ilbon'gun wianbu."

22   Bxx (pseudonym; b. 1927): *Tŭllinayo?*

23   Bxx (pseudonym; b. 1927): *Tŭllinayo?*

24 Kim Poktong.

25 Ch'oe Kapsun: *Kiŏg ŭro tashi ssŭnŭn yŏksa.*

26 Yi Sunak.

27 Kim Poktong.

28 Kim Tŏkchin: *Kangje ro kkŭllyŏgan Chosŏnin kun wianbu tŭl*, vol. 1.

29 Exx (pseudonym): *Tŭllinayo?*; Kim Ch'unhŭi: *Kangje ro kkŭllyŏgan Chosŏnin kun wianbu tŭl*, vol. 2.

30 Chang Chŏmdol: *Yŏksa rŭl mandŭnŭn iyagi.*

31 Pak Sunae: *Kangje ro kkŭllyŏgan Chosŏnin kun wianbu tŭl*, vol. 1.

32 Ch'oe Chŏngnye: *Kangje ro kkŭllyŏgan Chosŏnin kun wianbu tŭl*, vol. 2.

33 Kim Tŏkchin: *Kangje ro kkŭllyŏgan Chosŏnin kun wianbu tŭl*, vol. 1.

34 Yi Tŭngnam: *Kangje ro kkŭllyŏgan Chosŏnin kun wianbu tŭl*, vol. 1.

35 Chang Chŏmdol: *Yŏksa rŭl mandŭnŭn iyagi.*

36 Chin Kyŏngp'aeng: *Kangje ro kkŭllyŏgan Chosŏnin kun wianbu tŭl*, vol. 2.

37 Kim Poktong; Ch'oe Illye: *Kangje ro kkŭllyŏgan Chosŏnin kun wianbu tŭl*, vol. 2.

38 Kim Tŏkchin: *Kangje ro kkŭllyŏgan Chosŏnin kun wianbu tŭl*, vol. 1.

39 Kim Ch'unhŭi: *Kangje ro kkŭllyŏgan Chosŏnin kun wianbu tŭl*, vol. 2.

40 Kim Poktong.

41 Axx (pseudonym; b. 1930): *Tŭllinayo?*

42 Ch'oe Illye: *Kangje ro kkŭllyŏgan Chosŏnin kun wianbu tŭl*, vol. 2.

43 Yi Sangok: *Kangje ro kkŭllyŏgan Chosŏnin kun wianbu tŭl*, vol. 1.

44 Chang Chŏmdol: *Yŏksa rŭl mandŭnŭn iyagi.*

45 Kim Okchu: *Kangje ro kkŭllyŏgan Chosŏnin kun wianbu tŭl*, vol. 3.

46 Ixx (pseudonym).

47 Kxx (pseudonym; b. 1923): *Tŭllinayo?*

48 Hun halmŏni (Grandmother Hun): *Pŏryŏjin Chosŏn ŭi ch'ŏnyŏ tŭl* [Throwaway Korean maidens]. Chŏngshindae halmŏni wa hamkke hanŭn shimin moim, 2004.

CHAPTER 5

1 Pak Sunae: *Kangje ro kkŭllyŏgan Chosŏnin kun wianbu tŭl*, vol. 1.

2 Kim Okchu: *Kangje ro kkŭllyŏgan Chosŏnin kun wianbu tŭl*, vol. 3.

3 Cho Sundŏk: *Kangje ro kkŭllyŏgan Chosŏnin kun wianbu tŭl*, vol. 3.

4 Im Chŏngja: *Yŏksa rŭl mandŭnŭn iyagi.*

5 Kim Ch'unhŭi: *Kangje ro kkŭllyŏgan Chosŏnin kun wianbu tŭl*, vol. 2.

6 Im Chŏngja: *Yŏksa rŭl mandŭnŭn iyagi.*

7 Kang Muja: *Kangje ro kkŭllyŏgan Chosŏnin kun wianbu tŭl*, vol. 2.

8 Son P'anim: *Kangje ro kkŭllyŏgan Chosŏnin kun wianbu tŭl*, vol. 2.

9 Hwang Kŭmju: *Kangje ro kkŭllyŏgan Chosŏnin kun wianbu tŭl*, vol. 1.

10 Ch'oe Illye: *Kangje ro kkŭllyŏgan Chosŏnin kun wianbu tŭl*, vol. 2.

11 Kang Muja: *Kangje ro kkŭllyŏgan Chosŏnin kun wianbu tŭl*, vol. 2.

12 Yi Yŏngsuk: *Kangje ro kkŭllyŏgan Chosŏnin kun wianbu tŭl*, vol. 1.

13 Mun Okchu: *Kangje ro kkŭllyŏgan Chosŏnin kun wianbu tŭl*, vol. 1.

14 Yi Yŏngsuk: *Kangje ro kkŭllyŏgan Chosŏnin kun wianbu tŭl*, vol. 1.

15 Yi Yŏngsuk: *Kangje ro kkŭllyŏgan Chosŏnin kun wianbu tŭl*, vol. 1.

16 Ha Sunnyŏ: *Kangje ro kkŭllyŏgan Chosŏnin kun wianbu tŭl*, vol. 1.

17 Son P'anim: *Kangje ro kkŭllyŏgan Chosŏnin kun wianbu tŭl*, vol. 2.

18 Pak Turi: *Kangje ro kkŭllyŏgan Chosŏnin kun wianbu tŭl*, vol. 2.

19 Yi Sunok: *Kangje ro kkŭllyŏgan Chosŏnin kun wianbu tŭl*, vol. 1.

20 Yi Sunok: *Kangje ro kkŭllyŏgan Chosŏnin kun wianbu tŭl*, vol. 1.

21 Shim Taryŏn: *Kangje ro kkŭllyŏgan Chosŏnin kun wianbu tŭl*, vol. 3.

22 Ch'oe Illye: *Kangje ro kkŭllyŏgan Chosŏnin kun wianbu tŭl*, vol. 2.

23 Yi Oksŏn (b. 1925): CNN interview, December 29, 2015.

24 Ch'oe Chŏngnye: *Kangje ro kkŭllyŏgan Chosŏnin kun wianbu tŭl*, vol. 2.

25 Pak Yŏni: *Kangje ro kkŭllyŏgan Chosŏnin kun wianbu tŭl*, vol. 2.

26 Kim Ŭnjin: *Kangje ro kkŭllyŏgan Chosŏnin kun wianbu tŭl*, vol. 2.

27 Pak Yŏni: *Kangje ro kkŭllyŏgan Chosŏnin kun wianbu tŭl*, vol. 2.

28 Kim Poktong.

29 Mun P'ilgi: *Kangje ro kkŭllyŏgan Chosŏnin kun wianbu tŭl*, vol. 1.

30 Pak Yŏni: *Kangje ro kkŭllyŏgan Chosŏnin kun wianbu tŭl*, vol. 2.

31 Kxx (pseudonym, b. 1930).

32 Hwang Kŭmju: *Kangje ro kkŭllyŏgan Chosŏnin kun wianbu tŭl*, vol. 1.

33 Yi Sunok: *Kangje ro kkŭllyŏgan Chosŏnin kun wianbu tŭl*, vol. 1.

34 Kang Muja: *Kangje ro kkŭllyŏgan Chosŏnin kun wianbu tŭl*, vol. 2.

35 Kim Pongi: *Yŏksa rŭl mandŭnŭn iyagi.*

36 Pak Yŏni: *Kangje ro kkŭllyŏgan Chosŏnin kun wianbu tŭl*, vol. 2.

37 Ch'oe Kapsun: *Kiŏk ŭro tashi ssŭnŭn yŏksa.*

38 Hwang Kŭmju: *Kangje ro kkŭllyŏgan Chosŏnin kun wianbu tŭl*, vol. 1.

39 Chŏng Sŏun.

40 Ch'oe Kapsun: *Kiŏk ŭro tashi ssŭnŭn yŏksa.*

41 Chŏng Sŏun; Ch'oe Illye: *Kangje ro kkŭllyŏgan Chosŏnin kun wianbu tŭl*, vol. 2.

42 Kang Tŏkkyŏng: *Kangje ro kkŭllyŏgan Chosŏnin kun wianbu tŭl*, vol. 1.

43 Hwang Kŭmju: *Kangje ro kkŭllyŏgan Chosŏnin kun wianbu tŭl*, vol. 1.

44 Chŏn Kŭmhwa: *Kangje ro kkŭllyŏgan Chosŏnin kun wianbu tŭl*, vol. 2.

45 Cho Sundŏk: *Kangje ro kkŭllyŏgan Chosŏnin kun wianbu tŭl*, vol. 3.

46 Kim Ch'unhŭi: *Kangje ro kkŭllyŏgan Chosŏnin kun wianbu tŭl*, vol. 2.

47 Kim Poktong.

48 Mun Okchu: *Kangje ro kkŭllyŏgan Chosŏnin kun wianbu tŭl*, vol. 2.

49 Mun Okchu: *Kangje ro kkŭllyŏgan Chosŏnin kun wianbu tŭl*, vol. 2.

CHAPTER 6

1 Kim Kunja: "Nae ka sarainnŭn han" [As long as I live], testimony before the Hanguk kyoyug'wŏn, February 7, 1997.
2 Cxx (pseudonym): *Tŭllinayo?*
3 Yi Yongsu: *Kangje ro kkŭllyŏgan Chosŏnin kun wianbu tŭl*, vol. 1.
4 Ch'oe Illye: *Kangje ro kkŭllyŏgan Chosŏnin kun wianbu tŭl*, vol. 2.
5 Ch'oe Hwasŏn.
6 Ch'oe Hwasŏn.
7 Ch'oe Hwasŏn.
8 Han Oksŏn: *Yŏksa rŭl mandŭnŭn iyagi.*
9 Yi Yongnyŏ: *Kangje ro kkŭllyŏgan Chosŏnin kun wianbu tŭl*, vol. 1.
10 Ch'oe Chŏngnye: *Kangje ro kkŭllyŏgan Chosŏnin kun wianbu tŭl*, vol. 2.
11 Hwang Kŭmju: *Kangje ro kkŭllyŏgan Chosŏnin kun wianbu tŭl*, vol. 1.
12 Kim Punsŏn: *Kangje ro kkŭllyŏgan Chosŏnin kun wianbu tŭl*, vol. 2.
13 Kim Ŭigyŏng: photo essay, House of Sharing, Kwangju, Kyŏnggi Province, Korea.
14 Kxx (pseudonym; b. 1923): *Tŭllinayo?*
15 Kxx (pseudonym; b. 1923): *Tŭllinayo?*
16 Yi Sangok: *Kangje ro kkŭllyŏgan Chosŏnin kun wianbu tŭl*, vol. 1.

CHAPTER 7

1 Mun P'ilgi: *Kangje ro kkŭllyŏgan Chosŏnin kun wianbu tŭl*, vol. 1.
2 Mun P'ilgi: *Kangje ro kkŭllyŏgan Chosŏnin kun wianbu tŭl*, vol. 1.
3 Kim Haksun.
4 Kim Haksun.
5 Ch'oe Myŏngsun: *Kangje ro kkŭllyŏgan Chosŏnin kun wianbu tŭl*, vol. 1.
6 Kim Poktong; Kim Ŭnjin: *Kangje ro kkŭllyŏgan Chosŏnin kun wianbu tŭl*, vol. 2.
7 Kim Okchu: *Kangje ro kkŭllyŏgan Chosŏnin kun wianbu tŭl*, vol. 3; Ch'oe Myŏngsun: *Kangje ro kkŭllyŏgan Chosŏnin kun wianbu tŭl*, vol. 1.
8 Kim Ch'unhŭi: *Kangje ro kkŭllyŏgan Chosŏnin kun wianbu tŭl*, vol. 2.
9 Yi Oksŏn: CNN interview, December 29, 2015.
10 Kil Wŏnok: *Yŏksa rŭl mandŭnŭn iyagi.*
11 Kil Wŏnok: *Yŏksa rŭl mandŭnŭn iyagi.*

CHAPER 8

1 Pak Ch'asun: An Sehong, "Na nŭn Ilbon'gun sŏngnoye yŏtta 3hwa: Wianso nŭn Ilbon'gun ŭi kongjung pyŏnso yŏtta" [I was a sex slave of the Japanese military 3: The comfort station was the Japanese military's public toilet], internet posting, February 2, 2016.
2 Hwang Kŭmju: *Kangje ro kkŭllyŏgan Chosŏnin kun wianbu tŭl*, vol. 1.

3 Pak Yŏni: *Kangje ro kkŭllyŏgan Chosŏnin kun wianbu tŭl*, vol. 2.
4 Axx (pseudonym; b. 1930): *Tŭllinayo?*
5 Kxx (pseudonym; b. 1923): *Tŭllinayo?*
6 Ch'oe Kapsun: *Kiŏk ŭro tashi ssŭnŭn yŏksa.*
7 Ch'oe Kapsun: *Kiŏk ŭro tashi ssŭnŭn yŏksa.*
8 Ch'oe Kapsun: *Kiŏk ŭro tashi ssŭnŭn yŏksa.*
9 Kim Ch'unhŭi: *Kangje ro kkŭllyŏgan Chosŏnin kun wianbu tŭl*, vol. 2.
10 Yi Oksŏn: *Yŏksa rŭl mandŭnŭn iyagi.*
11 Ch'oe Kapsun: *Kiŏk ŭro tashi ssŭnŭn yŏksa.*
12 Ch'oe Chŏngnye: *Kangje ro kkŭllyŏgan Chosŏnin kun wianbu tŭl*, vol. 2; Ch'oe Kapsun: *Kiŏk ŭro tashi ssŭnŭn yŏksa.*
13 Ch'oe Illye: *Kangje ro kkŭllyŏgan Chosŏnin kun wianbu tŭl*, vol. 2.
14 Kim Kunja: "Nae ka sarainnŭn han."
15 Kang Muja: *Kangje ro kkŭllyŏgan Chosŏnin kun wianbu tŭl*, vol. 2.
16 Kim Yŏngja: *Kiŏk ŭro tashi ssŭnŭn yŏksa.*
17 Kim Sunak: *Nae sok ŭn amu to morŭndak'ai.*

CHAPTER 9

1 Kxx (pseudonym; b. 1923): *Tŭllinayo?*
2 Fxx (pseudonym): *Tŭllinayo?*
3 Ixx (pseudonym).
4 Ixx (pseudonym).
5 Hwang Suni: *Kangje ro kkŭllyŏgan Chosŏnin kun wianbu tŭl*, vol. 3.
6 Kxx (pseudonym; b. 1923): *Tŭllinayo?*
7 Kxx (pseudonym; b. 1923): *Tŭllinayo?*
8 Kxx (pseudonym; b. 1923): *Tŭllinayo?*
9 Kim Tŏkchin: *Kangje ro kkŭllyŏgan Chosŏnin kun wianbu tŭl*, vol. 1.
10 Hwang Suni: *Kangje ro kkŭllyŏgan Chosŏnin kun wianbu tŭl*, vol. 3.
11 Kil Wŏnok: *Yŏksa rŭl mandŭnŭn iyagi.*
12 Cho Sundŏk: *Kangje ro kkŭllyŏgan Chosŏnin kun wianbu tŭl*, vol. 3.
13 Cho Sundŏk: *Kangje ro kkŭllyŏgan Chosŏnin kun wianbu tŭl*, vol. 3.
14 Yi Yongsu: *Kangje ro kkŭllyŏgan Chosŏnin kun wianbu tŭl*, vol. 1.
15 Kim Hwasŏn: *Kiŏk ŭro tashi ssŭnŭn yŏksa.*
16 Kang Muja: *Kangje ro kkŭllyŏgan Chosŏnin kun wianbu tŭl*, vol. 2.
17 Kang Muja: *Kangje ro kkŭllyŏgan Chosŏnin kun wianbu tŭl*, vol. 2.
18 Kang Tŏkkyŏng: *Kangje ro kkŭllyŏgan Chosŏnin kun wianbu tŭl*, vol. 1.
19 Kim Poktong: "Nan p'yŏngsaeng chŏng iragon chuŏbon chŏk i ŏpta" [Never have I given my heart away], *Hangyŏre*, December 12, 2015.
20 Han Oksŏn: *Yŏksa rŭl mandŭnŭn iyagi.*

CHAPTER 10

1 Kim Ch'unhŭi: *Kangje ro kkŭllyŏgan Chosŏnin kun wianbu tŭl*, vol. 2.

2 Chang Chŏmdol: *Yŏksa rŭl mandŭnŭn iyagi.*

3 Chang Chŏmdol: *Yŏksa rŭl mandŭnŭn iyagi.*

4 Hwang Suni: *Kangje ro kkŭllyŏgan Chosŏnin kun wianbu tŭl*, vol. 3.

5 An Pŏpsun: *Kiŏk ŭro tashi ssŭnŭn yŏksa*; Im Chŏngja, *Yŏksa rŭl mandŭnŭn iyagi*; Kim Poktong: "Nyusŭmaegŏjin Shik'ago" broadcast, December 27, 2013.

6 Kim Poktong.

7 Mun Okchu: *Kangje ro kkŭllyŏgan Chosŏnin kun wianbu tŭl*, vol. 1.

8 Hwang Kŭmju: *Kangje ro kkŭllyŏgan Chosŏnin kun wianbu tŭl*, vol. 1.

CHAPTER 11

1 Kang Tŏkkyŏng: *Kangje ro kkŭllyŏgan Chosŏnin kun wianbu tŭl*, vol. 1.

2 Kim Ŭnjin: *Kangje ro kkŭllyŏgan Chosŏnin kun wianbu tŭl*, vol. 2.

3 Mun P'ilgi: *Kangje ro kkŭllyŏgan Chosŏnin kun wianbu tŭl*, vol. 1.

4 Chin Kyŏngp'aeng: *Kangje ro kkŭllyŏgan Chosŏnin kun wianbu tŭl*, vol. 2.

CHAPTER 12

1 Kim Poktong.

2 Yi Sudan.

3 Yi Sudan.

4 Hwang Suni: *Kangje ro kkŭllyŏgan Chosŏnin kun wianbu tŭl*, vol. 3.

CHAPTER 14

1 Kxx (pseudonym; b. 1923): *Tŭllinayo?*

2 Yun Sunman: *Kiŏk ŭro tashi ssŭnŭn yŏksa.*

3 Kim Poktong.

4 Kim Yŏngja: *Kiŏk ŭro tashi ssŭnŭn yŏksa.*

5 Kim Poktong: CNN interview, April 29, 2015.

6 Kim Haksun.

CHAPTER 15

1 Yi Yongsu: *Kangje ro kkŭllyŏgan Chosŏnin kun wianbu tŭl*, vol. 1.

2 Yi Yongsu: *Kangje ro kkŭllyŏgan Chosŏnin kun wianbu tŭl*, vol. 1.

3 Yi Oksŏn.

4 Yun Turi: *Kangje ro kkŭllyŏgan Chosŏnin kun wianbu tŭl*, vol. 1.

5 Zang Zhendu: "Kkŭnnajianŭn chŏnjaeng, Ilbon'gun wianbu."

CHAPTER 16

1 Zang Zhendu: "Kkŭnnajianŭn chŏnjaeng, Ilbon'gun wianbu."
2 Hwang Kŭmju: Yi Toŭn, "Ilbon'gun kkŭnnajianŭn iyagi" [The endless story of the Japanese military], YouTube.
3 Chŏng Oksun: "Chiok ŭi hyŏngbŏl poda tŏ ch'ittŏllinŭn Ilbon'gun ŭi manhaeng."
4 Kim Yŏngsuk: "Pukch'ŭk chonggun wianbu p'ihaeja Kim Yŏngsuk halmŏni chŭngŏn."
5 Yi Yongsu: interviews based on testimony by Yi Yongsu halmŏni in Washington, DC, April 21, 2015.
6 Yi Yongsu: interviews based on testimony by Yi Yongsu halmŏni in Washington, DC, April 21, 2015.
7 Mun Okchu: *Kangje ro kkŭllyŏgan Chosŏnin kun wianbu tŭl*, vol. 1.
8 Yi Okpun.
9 Axx (pseudonym; b. 1930): *Tŭllinayo?*
10 Pak Yŏni: *Kangje ro kkŭllyŏgan Chosŏnin kun wianbu tŭl*, vol. 2.
11 Mun Okchu: Morikawa Michiko, *Pŏmŏ chŏnsŏn Ilbon'gun "wianbu" Mun Okchu* [Mun Okchu, "comfort woman" for the Japanese military at the Burma front], trans. from the Japanese by Kim Chŏngsŏng. Chŏngshindae halmŏni wa hamkke hanŭn shimin moim, 2005.
12 Zang Zhendu: "Kkŭnnajianŭn chŏnjaeng, Ilbon'gun wianbu."
13 Yi Ch'i (an Indonesian comfort woman and victim of the Japanese military): "Kkŭnnajianŭn chŏnjaeng, Ilbon'gun wianbu" [Endless war, comfort women for the Japanese military], broadcast on "KBS p'anorama p'ŭllŏsŭ," August 11, 2013.

KIM SOOM was born in Ulsan, South Kyŏngsang Province, and earned a degree in social welfare from Taejŏn University. She first appeared in print in 1997 and has since published six story collections and nine novels. She is the recipient of the Hŏ Kyun (2012), Daesan (2013), Yi Sang (2015), and Tongni-Mogwŏl (2017) literary prizes as well as the 2017 Special Reunification Prize. *One Left* is her first novel to appear in English translation.

BRUCE AND JU-CHAN FULTON have translated numerous works of modern Korean fiction. Their awards and fellowships include the first US National Endowment for the Arts Translation Fellowship for a Korean project and an America PEN Heim Translation Grant for *One Left*. Bruce Fulton is the inaugural holder of the Young-Bin Min Chair in Korean Literature and Literary Translation and associate professor of Asian studies at the University of British Columbia.